Chicago Public Library

REFERENCE

Form 178 rev. 1-94

the MULTIDIMENSIONAL

M A N A G E R

24 WAYS TO IMPACT *your* BOTTOM LINE *in* 90 DAYS

Richard Connelly Ph.D., Robin McNeill, and Roland Mosimann

This book is dedicated to Tom Peters, Peter Drucker, Andrew Grove, and the many other brilliant management writers who have covered all the bases about improving business performance — except this one.

Published by Cognos Incorporated, 3755 Riverside Drive, P.O. Box 9707, Station T, Ottawa, ON, Canada, K1G 4K9.

Contents

Chapter 1

Introduction

Throughout business history, seemingly unknown companies have come out of nowhere to overtake established market leaders without appearing to even break into a sweat. As Peter Drucker points out in his classic *Harvard Business Review* article "The Information Executives Truly Need," the newcomer invariably enjoys a tremendous cost advantage, usually about 30 percent. The reason: the newcomer has a superior method of managing costs across the integrated supply chain to the customer.

In recent years, we have seen Drucker's phenomenon reenacted in a new breed of newcomer — innovative companies who have been able to cut costs and increase profitability at an explosive rate — breaking through to achieve a superior method of managing costs across their own supply chains.

What we learned from these companies is that they have brought about a significant change in the way they view their business models. They replaced the traditional emphasis on products and revenue with more *customer-* and *profit-centric* business models — a new and broader set of indicators that act to maximize the full profit potential of every customer.

One of their major discoveries, which we will share in this book, is that moving to these new business models requires an enabling technology. To shift an entire company to *customer-* and *profit-centric* business models required a technology that dispersed these new measurements quickly and cheaply. At the same time, a new breed of managers emerged. We'll call them *multidimensional managers* because they operate in a world that has become far too complex, too *multidimensional*, for decisions to be centralized or concentrated at the top.

In the next few pages, we will describe who multidimensional managers are, what they do, where they do it, and why many observers expect that all managers will become multidimensional managers in the next few years. But the most important thing to know about multidimensional managers is that they have unusual leverage on business performance. They are changing the way corporations operate: the way they sell, the way they interact with their customers and suppliers, and the way they align their management teams around financial goals.

And they can start to have this impact in 90 days.

In 1994, Howard Dresner, a top analyst for Gartner Group[1], made a remarkable prediction about manager behavior. Simultaneously, he named a new generation of software called *business intelligence*, superseding an earlier generation of software named *decision support*. Consulting with many Fortune 1000 companies, Dresner was in a unique position to see what leading-edge corporations and leading-edge technology suppliers were planning for the next 24 months. Based on those sources, Dresner foresaw a dramatic shift in the way large corporations would understand their business. Dresner predicted:

> *"By 1996, use of business intelligence solutions will shift dramatically away from dedicated analysts to all managers and professionals as the preferred way of understanding the business… Instead of a small number of analysts spending 100 percent of their time analyzing data, <u>all managers and professionals will spend 10 percent of their time using BI software.</u>"*

It was a remarkable prediction at the time and raised an obvious point. Managers are highly committed to their own personal productivity and so are the corporations that pay them. What would *compel all managers and professionals* to take up this new activity? There are only two rational explanations: either

2

[1]Gartner Group advises the Fortune 1000 on information technology.

this new activity offered a new level of contribution to corporate objectives that wasn't possible before, or this new activity sharply reduced other time previously spent getting the same results.

In fact, both explanations have proven to be true. The generation of software named *business intelligence* by Dresner allows corporations to *accelerate the rate at which managers can physically process information.*

The companies that were first to grasp this realization immediately began to display the dramatic shift in behavior that Dresner had predicted. The fact is that for most operational questions about business performance, it isn't faster to ask a dedicated analyst any more. It's faster and far less expensive per question to find out for yourself — if you're a multidimensional manager.

The majority of corporations did not pick up on Howard Dresner's prediction about business intelligence as quickly as he thought they would. In 1996, we aren't yet living in a world where all dedicated analysts have disappeared and all managers and professionals now spend 10 percent of their time using business intelligence software. But hundreds of leading-edge corporations did pick up on Dresner's prediction. Many of them are in this book. In these corporations, more than 250,000 managers and professionals have become multidimensional managers. Their numbers are more than doubling every year.

With this new breed of multidimensional managers, the companies in this book were able to *visibly, verifiably, and significantly reduce total operating costs, radically improve productivity in an already well-understood critical success factor, or enable previously unavailable strategic capabilities.* Often they were able to achieve all three.

Moreover, in our work with these companies, we have seen a *pattern of solutions* emerge as managers apply this new technology to their most immediate business problems. Corporation after corporation made the same discoveries. We began to realize that this pattern could apply to any company in the same industry. The discovery that improves sales performance in one company will have a similar impact for the next company. The discovery that shortens lead times in one company's manufacturing operation will have roughly the same outcome for another manufacturer.

We refer to this core pattern as the 24 Ways. They are the 24 Ways that multidimensional managers use to achieve great competitive advantage. The following pages are meant to save years of experimentation and potentially millions of dollars in getting these multidimensional managers in place.

Good luck with the 24 Ways and your new future as a multidimensional manager!

Chapter 2
The 90-Day Promise

The promise of *The Multidimensional Manager* is that you can gain strategic cost advantage and increase profits in your corporation — and see results in 90 days. To validate this promise, we will share the experiences of many successful, brand-name companies who have radically shifted their competitive position in very short time frames. Companies like Armstrong World Industries, which won the Baldridge Quality Award in 1995. Glaxo Wellcome. York International. Coors Brewing. Crown Cork & Seal. Analog Devices. Hamilton Beach/Proctor-Silex. All leading-edge companies in their respective industries. There is no substantive reason why any corporation cannot reproduce at least one of the Ways presented in this book within 90 days.

Unlike many ideas for improving business performance, the 24 Ways do not require you to declare a revolution in your company, change your leadership style, foster a new culture by edict, or consciously set out to reengineer the way people behave. People *will* behave differently. But they will hardly notice it happening because they are too busy getting results.

While observing these changes in management behavior, these companies realized — earlier than the rest of us — the critical importance of *mastering information*. They realized that despite owning powerful information about themselves, their suppliers, their carriers, and their customers, they had never had an efficient way to get this information to their management teams.

The 24 Ways demonstrate how these companies found new ways to master information and improve business performance

5

dramatically. But before you read on, there are three insights that are fundamental to grasping the full potential of the 24 Ways. These insights underlie the achievements of these companies and the promise of this book.

Insight #1: The Information "Sweet Spot"

The first insight is the idea of an information "sweet spot." If you think of the sweet spot found on a golf club, it's the point at which the energy from the swinging club is most forcefully and effectively transferred from the club face to the ball. Miss the sweet spot and the result is less distance and less accuracy. Hit the sweet spot with the same velocity, and watch the ball take off.

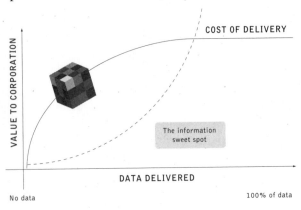

Insight #1: Some chunks of information are more important than others. These chunks, or "sweet spots," are, in fact, the 24 Ways.

This is the idea behind the information sweet spot insight: that the most valuable information for corporate decision-making is concentrated in a relatively small number of "sweet spots" in the information that flows through a corporation. By analyzing these sweet spots, you can drive up production, drive down costs, and drive the business towards more *customer-* and *profit-centric* business models.

This insight has significant practical implications. While prevailing wisdom suggests that managers need as much information as possible, the sweet spot insight reveals the importance of quality over quantity. Because these sweet spots are associated with *key manager activities*, managers are given the selective chunks of information that will help them react far more quickly and inexpensively than previously imagined to changing business conditions.

The 24 Ways in this book are, in fact, 24 "information sweet spots" discovered by world-class corporations. They are the chunks of information which have led to a new class of managers — *multidimensional managers*.

Insight #2: Managers Think Multidimensionally

Managers have a picture of the business in their minds that looks pretty much like the one shown below. Managers are not necessarily aware that they think multidimensionally, though in fact they do. They are forced to think multidimensionally because the numbers they are attempting to understand are generated by multiple interactions between customers, products, salespeople, and many other variables.

Insight #2: Managers think multidimensionally across all the potential combinations of salespeople, products, customers, and indicators.

The concept of multidimensional analysis is important to grasp because it turns out to be one of the primary challenges of business. Say in the example above, you have 10 salespeople who sell an average of 10 products to each of 100 customers every month, and the corporation tracks five key indicators. All the combinations of salespeople, products, months, customers, and indicators adds up to a sizable number.

10 salesreps x 10 products x 100 customers x 24 months x 5 indicators = 1,200,000 combinations

Delivering this information on paper is not very useful. Even at 50 lines a page, you would be reviewing a report equal in length to several dozen copies of Tolstoy's *War and Peace*. On the other hand, if managers cannot drill down to a significant level of detail, *they never see the real drivers of cost and margin*.

To accelerate their understanding of the business, managers need to receive information in a format that matches the way they think. They need to get information in a format where changing indicators is as easy as switching gears in a car. Where navigating through dimensions is as instinctive as finding their way home after work. Where they can make 20 important discoveries about why the business is on or off target — in seconds.

When managers bring this faster rate of processing information to carefully chosen "sweet spots" involved in key manager activities, they *remove information gathering as the limiting step* in performing these activities. They perform the activity at a higher rate, their output increases, and so does their impact on financial performance.

Insight #3: The Reporting Paradigm for Managers Has Changed

The reporting paradigm has changed. It is now based on business intelligence technology, which formats information multidimensionally — the way managers think. This format *accelerates the rate at which managers can physically process information*.

Multidimensional formats are not new, but business intelligence is. Business intelligence dramatically lowers the price point and shortens the time to get information into this key format. In 1994, the leading business intelligence software, a product called PowerPlay®, introduced a simple, low-cost method of transforming sweet spots of information into a multidimensional format for fast consumption by managers in critical locations across the supply chain. Entire sweet spots, now organized the way managers think, could be captured in "multidimensional reports" that took as little as one megabyte on a manager's laptop. A single multidimensional report might be equivalent to thousands of conventional reports represented on paper.

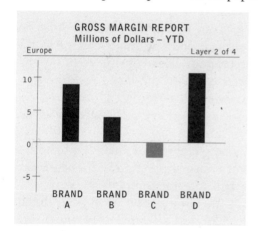

GROSS MARGIN REPORT
Millions of Dollars – YTD

Europe   Layer 2 of 4

WAY 7

All combinations
of salespeople,
customers,
products, and
indicators

A single "cube" is equivalent to thousands of conventional reports.

These new multidimensional reports could literally contain all the 1,200,000 combinations in the earlier example. Managers could explore any of the combinations in seconds using a multi-dimensional viewer. They could instantly compare the results of one combination with any other combination, trend the results of any combination over time, and zero in on which factors were driving their key indicators.

Corporations quickly saw the real cost that this new paradigm eliminated: the cost of working with information. This cost is rarely tracked; no line item on the income statement indicates "cost of working with information." But many observers now consider it the largest single hidden cost of corporate operations.

One recent activity-based costing and benchmarking study captures the magnitude of the issue. The study was completed in April 1996 by Maritime Tel & Tel (MT&T), the $400 million supplier of telephone services in eastern Canada.

The study measured the cost of working with financial information — independent of fixed investment such as computers, financial software, networks, or the systems that collect and store financial data. It discovered that the cost to create, distribute, and work with the company's financial reports alone was several million dollars a year.

This MT&T example is one of the first clear quantifications of the uncaptured, untracked, and enormous cost of working with information in corporations. This cost is layered on top of every product and service a company produces. So is the cost of every salesrep's business review that requires a week to prepare instead of an hour. So is the cost of every HR report that takes days to prepare instead of minutes.

The new reporting paradigm eliminates many of these costs. Managers can now master information in powerful new ways to drive down costs across their integrated supply chains.

These three insights — the information sweet spot, thinking multidimensionally, and adopting a reporting paradigm based on business intelligence technology — form the basis of the 90-day promise. The 24 Ways are the *how* and *where* of applying these insights. They capture the points along the integrated supply chain where business intelligence can have the most impact on the bottom line in the shortest amount of time. They support key manager activities that have a disproportionate impact on the financial statements.

Each of the 24 Ways is fully explained in this book. Anyone can adopt them. Any corporation can adopt at least one of the 24 Ways and improve business performance in 90 days.

Chapter 3

The 24 Ways

The top request we get from major corporations is to share with them what we have learned about achieving maximum competitive advantage with multidimensional managers. This book, the chart below, and the 24 Ways are our attempt to respond in the most efficient and practical way possible. But you will quickly see that everything we have learned comes back to a single theme — you maximize profitability when everybody in the company is managing it. One division head at Glaxo Wellcome understood exactly what multidimensional managers could do for his organization. As he declared to his division: "I'm tired of managing profitability by myself. Now you're going to do it!" The 24 Ways in this book inevitably drive organizations to that outcome.

As we said in chapter one, some "chunks" of information are more important than others — the sweet spot insight. The 24 Ways are, in fact, the chunks of information that have the most impact on profitability. Where did these 24 Ways come from? They come from creative, innovative corporations that have experienced breakthroughs in cost reduction, quality, customer satisfaction, and profitability. The examples we present here are the most successful patterns we have seen, repeated in company after company.

There are other sweet spots that can have a big impact on a corporation. No doubt there are limitless ways that can be invented and an endless set of extensions that will continue to add value over time. The 24 Ways, however, are the tried and true sweet spots, the surest and fastest way to align a management team around strategic cost advantage and profitability.

Presented visually, a table of contents for the 24 Ways lines up against the major functional departments in a manufacturing organization. Each of the 24 Ways is associated with a department. Each department has between one and five sweet spots, mapping the key business functions that drive profitability.

24 Ways To Impact Your Business in 90 Days

GENERAL MANAGEMENT

Finance	HR/IT
1 Multidimensional Income Statement	21 HR Administration
2 Profit Drill-Down Analysis	22 Core Competence Inventory
3 Multidimensional Balance Sheet	23 BI Deployment
4 Key Financial Ratios	24 24 Ways ROI
5 Cash Flow Analysis	

Sales	Marketing	Purchasing	Production	Distribution	Customer Service
6 Sales Analysis	10 Strategic Marketing Analysis	12 Inventory Turnover	14 Capacity Management	17 Carrier Scorecard	18 On-Time Delivery
7 Customer & Product Profitability	11 Tactical Marketing Analysis	13 Supplier Scorecard	15 Standard Product Cost & Quality		19 Complaints, Returns, & Claims
8 Sales Plan vs. Forecast			16 Cause of Poor Quality		20 Cost of Service Relationship
9 Sales Pipeline					

At the conceptual level, the chart might look more like the diagram below. If you imagine information as oil in a pipeline, each of the 24 Ways is a substation that monitors the flow of information.

The 24 Ways are like monitoring stations along the flow of information, capturing the sweet spots that impact profitability.

As you will notice, the stations, or sweet spots, are pictured as cubes. That's the way multidimensional information tends to be shown. Each of the six faces of the cube is a dimension, a fundamental way of categorizing the business. In fact, some sweet spots have more than six dimensions, some have less. But six is a good average — which is why cubes have come to represent information structured multidimensionally. Each cube is a multidimensional picture of the business, a highly efficient monitoring station for managers to understand what is driving their part of the business, and more particularly, what is driving their contribution to profitability.

The chapters of this book reflect the stucture of a manufacturing business, which in turn mirrors the flow of products and services across the supply chain. We've chosen manufacturing to illustrate the 24 Ways because it's the most general model of a business. The underlying business issues in the 24 Ways, however, apply to any corporation or government organization.

You will also notice, as you proceed through *The Multidimensional Manager*, that each of the 24 Ways points directly back to the financial statements. These documents are typically viewed as the preserve of the finance department, often difficult for the average person to interpret. Few of us can look at an income statement, balance sheet, or cash flow statement with anything approaching passion. Financial statements obviously have importance to the bank and to the investor community, but what role do they play in the day-to-day life of operational managers?

Each of the 24 Ways points back to the financial statements.

A great deal, argues Jack Stack in *The Great Game of Business*. Stack's central argument is that the more people become aware of their direct impact on the financial statements, the better they will perform. When all managers work from the same report cards — the income statement, the cash flow statement, and the balance sheet — they all know exactly what they contribute, what they cost the company, and how they depend on one another to be successful. They also stay focused on the overall success of the business.

The added insight in *The Multidimensional Manager* is that in reality, the financial statements are multidimensional documents. If you could drill down far enough, ultimately you would arrive at products, customers, quality, and customer satisfaction — the real drivers of cost and profit. With the 24 Ways, that is exactly what happens.

 Each of the 24 Ways points back to individual line items on the income statement and balance sheet. The key performance indicators in these sweet spots drive the associated line items in the financial statements. Now, instead of *looking at* the financial statements, multidimensional managers are *working in them*. They are managing compact universes of critical success factors at high-leverage pressure points on the supply chain. The cost of working with this high-leverage information is largely eliminated, so they can see which specific factors are driving margin or cost. And they can make the direct connection to the report card published quarterly by the company to its shareholders.

This is the pattern of the 24 Ways. And the outcome is an organization where everyone manages profitability.

Chapter 4

Reinventing Analysis in Finance

"Managerial productivity — that is, the output of a manager per unit of time worked — can be increased in three ways:

- *Increasing the rate with which a manager performs his activities, speeding up his work.*
- *Increasing the leverage associated with the various managerial activities.*
- *Shifting the mix of a manager's activities from those with lower to those with higher leverage."*

— *Andrew S. Grove, High Output Management*

What Finance Sees ... and Doesn't See

Most analysis in corporations is concentrated in the finance department. Finance has the best overall view of the business. It gets the consolidated numbers from all operations. It is also the place in the business where concern for profit, cash flow, and the strength of the balance sheet is greatest. So it is natural that a great deal of analysis occurs there. Financial analysis is a highly leveraged activity. It captures all costs, all revenues, and all performance against expectation, and presents primary feedback to management for corrective action across the business. It is performed by people with a critical eye who understand exactly how the board and the banks see the numbers — and how the investment community will subsequently value them.

Unfortunately, the traditional practice of analysis in finance is less than optimal for three reasons:

Reason 1. Most of the analysis in corporations is concentrated in the finance department.

Some 85–95 percent of managers who are not in finance have direct accountability for 100 percent of the business. Operational managers in operational departments have the best understanding of their own numbers, yet when it comes to analysis, they are often left out in the cold.

Reason 2. The finance department sees only a limited slice of the business.

Financial systems are built around the chart of accounts as the primary dimension, as shown below. If we drew a map of the information that most finance departments extract from these systems to report and analyze performance, it would look like this:

TIME PERIODS	FINANCIAL STATEMENTS	ORGANIZATION	INDICATORS
Years	**Income Statement**	Divisions	**Income Statement**
– – – – –	Revenue	– – – – –	Plan
Quarters	COGS	Departments	Actual
– – – – –	Gross Profit		Variance
Months	SG&A		% Variance
	Operating Profit		Rolling Forecast
	Interest		**Balance Sheet**
	Net Profit		Opening Balance
	Balance Sheet		Closing Balance
	Cash Flow		Net Change

The major business dimensions that drive cost and margin — such as product and customer — typically are not in the finance department's picture of events. Also, the balance sheet and cash flow line items often are not broken down by organizational units.

Where are the product and customer dimensions that drive cost and margin? They aren't in the picture. Instead, finance sees a time dimension to track progress during the year, a dimension for the chart of accounts to record revenues and expenses in accounting categories, and a dimension for the organizational units in the company. Given the boundaries of this information, the vision of finance is severely limited. Finance can certainly see who is on plan and who isn't. It can capture all the high-level financial indicators and compare them to industry benchmarks. It can present variances between performance and expectation to management, the board, and the bank. But finance can only *suspect* what is driving those variances. It cannot *pinpoint* the real issues or opportunities that drive profitability and cash, because product, customer, and other important dimensions are not included in this limited picture of the business.

Reason 3. Only a tiny percentage of analysis in the finance department actually is analysis.

Finance often functions as a "production shop," where financial analysts spend most of their time consumed by end-of-period reporting. They produce the same reports and answer the same variations on the same questions every month, quarter, and year-end. Finance is chained to galley oars as the ship plows through the seas. From such a position, it is difficult to see beyond the horizon.

Can this really be the situation in finance? As we have said, finance sees only a limited view of the business. But even in this limited picture, an enormous number of combinations and intersections exists. Consider a relatively small operating division with 200 cost centers and 500 expense accounts. That's 100,000 combinations and permutations.

TIME PERIODS	FINANCIAL STATEMENTS	ORGANIZATIONAL UNITS	INDICATORS
Months 12	Expense Accounts 500	Cost Centers 200	Indicators 6

12 x 500 x 200 x 6 = 7.2 million possible combinations

The reality for finance: 7.2 million possible answers every month.

Since all this activity is reported monthly, and we are interested in yearly trends, the figure increases 12-fold to 1.2 million combinations. This is for one indicator. Assume a minimum of at least six. That adds up to 7.2 million combinations. What if you had 5,000 expense accounts, not just 500? You start to understand what it is like to be in finance at the close of every month.

The finance department is consumed by reporting these numbers. Their tools are the programmed reports from the financial systems and spreadsheets. Many of the numbers from these programmed reports must be typed manually into spreadsheets to derive key ratios. Days of "analysis" are spent generating standard reports for internal and external requirements. Any time left over is spent answering ad hoc questions on the same subject matter. Often finance cannot respond quickly to these ad hoc questions, and its service reputation suffers. The process repeats itself monthly, quarterly, and annually.

In short, the return on investment from financial analysis activity is much lower than it should be — much lower than corporations suspect. And that limits their profit potential.

Freeing Up Finance

The sweet spots of information defined in this chapter dramatically increase the rate at which finance performs analysis. The statement, "we cut analysis time in finance from man-days to minutes," from the finance department at Epson, is typical.

Part of the reason is *simplification*: a large number of steps in assembling paper reports and rekeying information into spreadsheets are eliminated. As well, these sweet spots represent *a single set-up* (in manufacturing terms), and replace a welter of different approaches to the task. They also represent a *common base of information*, accessible instantly to everyone on the finance team.

Speeding up its work frees up finance. Increasing the leverage of its work frees up finance even more. York International provides an example of how a corporation can distribute these sweet spots of financial information directly to operational managers, who then perform their own reporting and analysis. With this approach, York's finance department freed up between one and two weeks monthly that had been consumed in repetitious report creation.

Sweet spots are created once, distributed to the rest of the organization, and refreshed with updated information automatically — as soon as period-end results are final. Finance increases the leverage of its work by changing the nature of its activity from analysis and report creation to information distribution.

York International, Epson, and hundreds of other corporations following their lead have solved the analysis problem with the 7.2 million combinations described above. They've solved it by becoming multidimensional managers. They've increased the rate at which they consume information within the finance department. They have removed themselves largely from the role of middlemen in the monthly reporting cycle, freeing enormous amounts of time in their departments for activities like value-added analysis. They have aggressively promoted extensive multidimensional analysis in their corporations. And they have encouraged operational managers to do their own reporting and analysis based on "sweet spots" provided by finance as well as other 24 Ways sweet spots that monitor the real drivers of cost and margin contained in other operational systems.

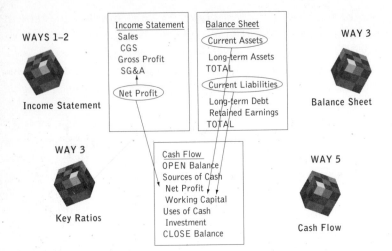

There are five classic sweet spots of information for finance. They transform the company's financial statements from paper into five multidimensional "cubes" for high-speed exploration. They are organized for easiest consumption internally in finance and for easiest distribution to other members of the management team.

Way 1 — Multidimensional Income Statement

"We cut analysis time in finance from man-days to minutes."
— *Epson America, Inc.*

Multidimensional Income Statement is a quick, compact summary of the income statement, primarily for the finance department. It includes a sufficient number of total line items to capture all the reports that are the backbone of the monthly and quarterly financial management review process. It might cover 20 high-level line items and several indicators across 600 departments and 12 months — still representing close to 100,000 combinations.

MATERIALS COST BY DIVISION (Materials as % of Cost of Goods Sold)				
Division 3				Layer 4 of 7
	Q1	Q2	Q3	Q4
Materials	41%	41%	43%	45%
Conversion	56%	56%	54%	52%
Shipping	3%	3%	3%	3%
Cost of Goods Sold	100%	100%	100%	100%

WAY 1

Quick, multidimensional exploration of the income statement reveals key trends, reports actual results against targets, and compares key ratios against industry benchmarks.

The information contained in this sweet spot speeds understanding of strategic trends, such as changes in cost structure. Often, the most valuable information is not simply how much the business spent on raw materials, but rather, how much the business spent on raw materials *in relation* to the total cost of goods sold. Multidimensional managers in finance can instantly trace and grasp shifts in cost structure at any operational level over any time period without rekeying information into spreadsheets.

Just as quickly, they can track performance at any level against business plan targets. They can track key income statement ratios such as operating margins against benchmark ratios for their industry. If any trend — or any key ratio — is going off track, they can dive down into deeper levels of the operation to find out what is driving the deviation.

Way 1, *Multidimensional Income Statement*, is most finance managers' first experience of what Epson calls the "man-days to minutes" productivity gain in their analysis activity. This sweet spot is used heavily as the new medium for "flash reporting" to speed period-end closings. New interim results may be broadcast several times as results are being finalized. Managers can immediately review the potential impact of revenue-recognition,

21

accrual, and deferral decisions. Once results are final, the majority of monthly reporting for senior management can be accomplished with Way 1.

Way 2 — Profit Drill-Down Analysis

"Like most businesses, our operational managers saw their numbers for the first time on day seven, when the accounting cycle closed. Then they'd analyze their variances, so all the adjustments would go through the following month. In one year, we moved to a position where all the operational managers' analysis is done, and their adjustments have gone through, <u>before we close on day seven.</u>"

— *PTT Telecom BV*

The second sweet spot, *Profit Drill-Down Analysis*, is designed for detailed expense and variance analysis at the lowest levels of operational planning. Here, the object of attention is the variance between actual expenses and plan for every category of expenditure and every cost center in the operating plan. Again, the possible combinations climb exponentially. With three indicators — actual, plan, and variance — 200 categories of expenditure, and 500 cost centers over 12 months, an analyst is looking at over 350,000 combinations.

This cost-center-level analysis is a key activity for enforcing planning discipline, capturing bottom-up changes in requirements or supplier prices that were not anticipated, and checking the accuracy of the numbers. *Profit Drill-Down Analysis* dramatically increases the speed at which finance can perform this activity. In particular, the sweet spot includes an "exception dimension" that highlights high variances and low variances. Financial analysts can zero in on the highest or lowest variances as a group and concentrate solely on them.

Far greater leverage is realized when the finance department distributes this detailed analysis to the operational managers who are actually in charge of cost centers. In fact, this process can have a material impact on the accuracy of information that supports ongoing decisions. Consider the experience of PTT Telecom, the Dutch telephone company. When operational managers saw their numbers for the first time on day seven of the month, the accounting cycle had closed. The operational managers then did their variance analysis, submitted their adjustments, and all adjustments went through in the following month. In the meantime, decisions about operational planning and forecasting went forward based on numbers that did not reflect the adjustments.

Today the situation is very different. The same operational managers now receive a sweet spot of their numbers on the 30th day of the closing month. Over the next seven days, they analyze the numbers and submit adjustments four to five times using daily updates of their sweet spots. When the accounting cycle closes on day seven, all the analysis has been done. All the adjustments for the month have gone through. Now they can concentrate on operational planning and forecasting for the next month, and base their business decisions on accurate numbers.

Reengineering the monthly reporting cycle: departments answer their own questions using distributed sweet spots. The managers who are directly accountable for results now share in the analysis. Finance is freed up for more value-added analysis.

At the same time, finance spends less time in the monthly reporting cycle because it no longer plays the middleman. Instead of producing countless reports and answering countless variations on the same questions every month, finance essentially pushes a button that refreshes the information in the cubes it distributes to operational management.

With the two weeks that York International's finance department has freed up, the company has been able to drive profitability analysis to a far deeper level of the business, leveraging many of the other 24 Ways in this book.

Way 3 — Multidimensional Balance Sheet

"As we move towards a more entrepreneurial culture, our executives need to become more involved in balance sheet concerns. We want them analyzing their own balance sheets, looking at their own debt-to-equity ratios and quick ratios as subsidiaries — so they can take this all into account as they plan capital requirements for their operation."

—*Titan Industrial Corporation*

A balance sheet is also a multidimensional document. A mere 100 balance sheet accounts across 24 months offers a formidable barrier to easy understanding and analysis. At the consolidated level, across 50 or 100 operating divisions, the barrier is exponentially compounded. Originally, Titan Industrial created this balance sheet sweet spot to provide more detailed capital-allocation analysis. This sweet spot accelerated the process of balance sheet reconciliation in finance enough to enable another strategic activity in Titan's business plan.

Titan wanted to strengthen and deepen its executives' financial understanding of the business so they could manage subsidiary operations with the broadest entrepreneurial scope. Way 3 provided the balance sheet side of the business in a medium that subsidiary managers could comprehend easily without requiring the overhead of dedicated financial analysis. As a result, the subsidiary senior executives could follow quick ratios and liquidity ratios at their level of the business, and contribute to key decisions on capital allocation that used to be made exclusively at a corporate level.

Way 3 often has associated sweet spots for detailed analysis of Accounts Receivable and Accounts Payable.

Way 4 — Key Financial Ratios

"There's one key measurement that we all watch in the company. But there are at least 25 other indicators and ratios that drive it. So we have to study them too, for all our operating divisions and sales distribution channels. We also have to trend them across five years of operations. We needed a simple way to do it."

— *Gordon Khan, Vice President of Finance,*
York International Corporation, Unitary Products Group

Way 4, *Key Financial Ratios*, packages the most important financial ratios for the business in a single sweet spot, along with the key underlying indicators that drive those ratios. In York International, for example, the discipline of the organization is driven by a single measurement — Adjusted Earnings Before Interest and Taxes (Adjusted EBIT).

It is a simple and powerful concept. Instead of being measured by revenue or even profit, York managers are measured on how much profit they generate *based on how much cash they had tied up to generate it*. In other words, York managers are

25

continually assessed on the return they generate from the capital they employ versus the cost of capital.

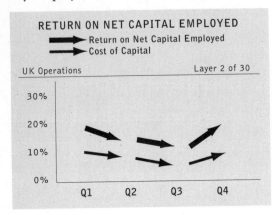

The cost of capital line shows the return that could have been generated by keeping the money in the bank. The Return on Net Capital Employed line shows how the management team performed in comparison.

Adjusted EBIT is, in turn, driven by a number of underlying financial ratios that reveal where capital is employed — in plant, property, equipment, inventory, accounts receivable, and so on. York bundles these ratios together in the *Key Financial Ratios* sweet spot. York managers then have a specially packaged sweet spot that supports them in achieving their fundamental goals for the corporation and maximizing their own compensation.

Way 5 — Cash Flow Analysis

"I couldn't distinguish on a regular basis who was impacting our profitability among all our subdivisions and sales organizations. Now every month I can tell at a glance which ones are providing or using cash."
— *Gordon Khan, Vice President of Finance,*
York International Corporation, Unitary Products Group

A financial officer is always trying to second-guess what demands on cash are coming next. Way 5 takes a lot of risk out of the balancing act. As Gordon Khan describes it, "With Way 5, I can quickly glance at our key operating indicators for various operations, subdivisions, and sales organizations. I choose which operations or subdivisions I want to check on, and then choose the indicators for working capital or gross profit. I get a picture of which operations or subdivisions are providing or using cash."

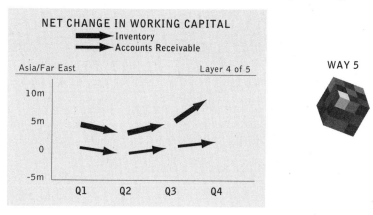

Asia/Far East is consuming higher rates of cash in both inventory and accounts receivable.

In Summary

York International, Epson, Titan Industrial, and other companies like them have redesigned the analysis activity in finance. They now perform analysis at a much faster rate, reducing days of reconciliation and reporting to minutes every month. Moreover, they have introduced a new and highly leveraged activity — information distribution. This latter activity removes finance from the role of middleman, eliminating hundreds of repetitive interactions with operational managers. It frees up days, even weeks of finance's time every reporting cycle. At the same time, it eliminates many steps in paper distribution and handling with all their attendant costs. The impact is to *visibly, verifiably, and significantly* reduce current overall *operating costs.*

To move their organizations to more *customer-* and *profit-centric* business models, the finance departments of these corporations have also aggressively sponsored the creation of other information sweet spots, the most popular of which are described in the next chapter.

Way 1 — Multidimensional Income Statement

TIME PERIODS	INCOME STMT. LINES	ORGANIZATIONS	% OF PLAN	INDICATORS
Years	Statement Classes	Divisions	> 120%	Plan
– – – – –	Revenue	– – – – –	111–120%	Actual
Quarters	COGS	Departments	100–110%	Rolling Forecast
– – – – –	SG&A		90–99%	Plan Variance
Months	Other Inc./Exp.		< 90%	% Plan
	Tax			% of RF
	– – – – – – – –			
	Statement Lines			

The first taste of "man-days to minutes" time savings in finance. All the high-level income statement trends and deviations from plan are captured here.

Way 2 — Profit Drill-Down Analysis

TIME PERIODS	INCOME STMT. LINES	ORGANIZATIONS	% OF PLAN	INDICATORS
Years	**Revenue**	Divisions	> 120%	Plan
	Sales	– – – – –	111–120%	Actual
Quarters	Discounts	Departments	100–110%	Rolling Forecast
– – – – –	**COGS**	Sales	90–99%	Plan Variance
Months	Materials	Marketing	< 90%	% Plan
– – – – –	Conversion	Purchasing		% of RF
	Shipping	Production		
	SG&A	Distribution		
	Selling	Customer Service		
	General	Human Resources		
	Administration	IT		
	Other Inc./Expense	Administration		
	Taxes			

The sweet spot for in-depth analysis of the expense lines driving gross profit and operating profit. Subsets are distributed directly to accountable managers to off-load monthly reporting from finance.

Way 3 — Multidimensional Balance Sheet

TIME PERIODS	BALANCE SHEET LINES	ORGANIZATIONS	% OF PLAN	INDICATORS
Years	**Statement Classes**	Company	**> 120%**	Opening Bal. (Act.)
– – – –	Assets	– – – – –	**111–120%**	Closing Bal. (Act.)
Quarters	Liabilities	Division	**100–110%**	Net Change (Act.)
– – – –	Retained Earnings		**90–99%**	Opening Bal. (Plan)
Months	– – – –		**< 90%**	Closing Bal. (Plan)
	Class Periods			Net Change (Var.)
	Short Term			
	Long Term			
	– – – –			
	Balance Sheet Lines			

Balance sheet line items are broken down by the contributing operating divisions here.

Way 4 — Key Financial Ratios

TIME PERIODS	ORGANIZATIONS	FINANCIAL INDICATORS	INDICATORS
Years	Company	EPS	Actual
– – – –	– – – – –	P/E	Plan
Quarters	Divisions	Quick Ratio	Rolling Forecast
– – – –		EBIT %	
Months		NCE %	
		RONCE	
		Return on Assets	
		AR %	
		Inventory %	
		PPE %	
		Working Cap. %	

The key ratios of most interest to the board, the bank, and the investment community are packaged here for the management team.

Way 5 — Cash Flow Analysis

TIME PERIODS	ORGANIZATIONS	CASH FLOW	INDICATORS
Years	Company	**Sources of Funds**	Net Change (Act.)
– – – –	– – – – –	Operating Lines	Net Change (Plan)
Quarters	Divisions	Investment Lines	Net Change
– – – –		**Uses of Funds**	(Rolling Forecast)
Months		Debt Repayment	
		Investment Lines	
		Other Activities	

Way 5 captures the complete cash picture for the CFO — is cash in the right places and at the right levels for the best return?

Back to the Financial Statements

Income Statement
   Revenue
   COGS
   Gross Profit
   SG&A
   Net Profit
   Interest

WAYS 1–5

Ways 1–5 impact the two major expense lines on the income statement. They reduce the Cost of Goods Sold [1] as a percentage of sales by involving line mangers in analyzing their own costs. They reduce SG&A [2] as a percentage of sales by increasing return on the finance component of SG&A and involving other SG&A line managers in the direct analysis of their costs.

Chapter 5

Aligning the Sales Force with Corporate Goals

"Achieving the full profit potential of each customer relationship should be the fundamental goal of every business…Yet the implicit business models that drive decisions in most large companies today do not focus on achieving this full profit potential."

— *Grant & Schlesinger, Harvard Business Review, Sept.+Oct. 1995*

What's Wrong in Sales

There are two obvious things wrong in most sales organizations. Both can have a significant negative impact on sales force performance. Both apply across the entire sales organization, and therefore impact between 20 and 40 percent of all employees. Even more important, both are barriers to adopting *customer-* and *profit-centric* business models.

Barrier 1. The goals of the sales force and the corporation are not fully aligned.

Most sales forces are still motivated by a *revenue*-centric, not a *profit*-centric view of the world. In the compensation plan, a dollar of revenue that earned 80 percent gross margin is worth the same as a dollar of revenue that earned 10 percent gross margin. Most organizations have no financial incentive to push revenue generation toward higher-margin dollars. Ironically, manufacturing companies go to considerable effort to establish a *standard product cost* for everything they manufacture. It is relatively easy to apply a standard product cost to any sales transaction and thereby calculate the gross margin impact of every transaction. But this valuable information has no visibility to the sales force. Even if salespeople — simply as good corporate citizens — wanted to focus their energy on higher-margin dollars, they would have no way of knowing which dollars earn the higher premium.

Barrier 2. The cost of working with information cripples productivity.

This is more than an efficiency issue; it has strategic impact. As we have stated earlier, the primary business process in sales is a conversation about *who* has sold *what* to *whom* and *when*. Typically, the process looks something like this:

150 CUSTOMERS 20 Products 30 Time Periods 6 Indicators	30 CUSTOMERS 20 Products 30 Time Periods 6 Indicators	1 CUSTOMER 20 Products 30 Time Periods 6 Indicators
DISTRICT MANAGER 250,000 combinations	SALESPERSON 50,000 combinations	CUSTOMER 2,500 combinations

A single salesperson's universe illustrates the primary productivity issue in sales — how to talk to a customer or a sales manager efficiently.

Conversations with a customer easily involve upwards of 2,500 combinations of facts. A conversation with a manager involves upwards of 50,000 combinations. It's no exaggeration to say that the average salesperson and sales manager spend weeks each year preparing business reviews and management reports on actual sales, forecast sales, and pipeline sales. The simplest analysis using paper reports and spreadsheets can take hours, even days.

Stated plainly, any attempt to analyze and present sales information in most sales organizations takes too much time. This heavy cost penalty obviously increases operating costs on a daily basis. But strategically, the penalty is far greater. The company misses opportunities to evolve the sales process in two critical directions.

The first lost opportunity is *fact-based selling*, which simply cannot get off the ground in a paper and spreadsheet world. Fact-based selling is a proven strategic advantage. The idea here is to "out-inform" both the buyer and competitors by using a company's own sales information — to support compelling sales propositions in face-to-face selling. There are endless factual selling stories in the data. A sales force leveraging its information in this way has a clear advantage over competitors who are not.

The second lost opportunity is *customer and product profitability*. This new business model only works if the sales force can dive and swim with fluidity in the universe of 50,000 combinations pictured above. We are now talking about the growth, trend, and mix of products sold to every customer. In particular, the sales force has to be able to assemble *product mix by customer* instantly — shown as either revenue or gross margin. Now they can focus on the key issue — the relative profit contribution of each of the products in the mix and how they can direct the business toward the most profitable mix. This game requires high-speed, flexible navigation through sales information at almost no cost. Any sales force that pays a high price every time it touches its sales information can't afford to play.

Reengineering the Conversation in Sales

The five Ways in this chapter are classics. They have transformed the selling process in thousands of companies ranging in size from leaders in the Fortune 100 to $100 million manufacturers. They dramatically simplify the work of understanding and communicating what is happening in a world of 5,000 or 50,000 or 500,000 combinations of facts. They remove the barriers that prevent companies from adopting *fact-based* selling and *profit-centric* selling. They transform unworkable information into competitive advantage.

Premier Beverages, a division of Dr Pepper/Seven Up, found that after a four-hour training session, their salespeople could suddenly see and analyze their unit sales by product and customer. They could answer customers' questions on the spot. Not only was the capability of the sales force improved, each salesperson saved days in information gathering every month.

For another well-known Fortune 100 corporation, "there was no other way we could have put yesterday's order volumes — plus month-to-date plan, forecast, rolling forecast, and stretch forecast — on our account managers' desks by 8:30 a.m. the next day *and* have them absorb all that information by 9:30 a.m." This corporation compresses tens of thousands of facts into 1–5 MB sweet spots that it e-mails to every account team at dawn. From that point, the account teams are self-contained. The answers to their questions are on their laptops. They're mobile. And the information takes almost no space on their laptops.

The first sweet spot in this chapter — *Sales Analysis* — is where most corporations begin. An eye-opener for both the sales organization and finance, this sweet spot is built from sales order information, which is readily available in most companies. As a result, any manufacturer can prototype *Sales Analysis* within a day or two — a week at most. Invariably, at least part of a corporation's sales force is in production within 90 days.

Way 6 — Sales Analysis

"Using Business Intelligence, our 200-person sales force reduced its forecast preparation time from six days to hours. This means we've gained 1,000 selling days every quarter."

— *Glaxo Wellcome*

Sales Analysis is a classic because it is so obviously a multi-dimensional solution, and because it satisfies such an urgent requirement in sales organizations. For the first time, everyone from the top to the bottom of the organization can see what is driving the business.

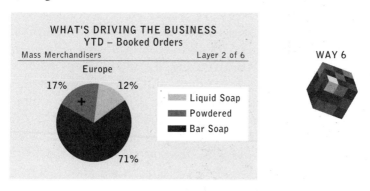

Bar soap dominates Mass Merchandiser business in Europe.

The "80-20 rule" jumps out in pie charts and bar charts. Multidimensional managers with *Sales Analysis* instantly see which product lines have the momentum. If one product line dominates the pie chart, they can "drill down" on the big slice to find out which specific products are driving the performance of the entire line. They can dive anywhere in the product dimension, anywhere in the sales territory dimension, anywhere in the customer dimension. They can isolate a major customer and then "slice" the overall customer revenue by product to see which products are driving the business in that account. They can compare the product story for that major customer with the story for any other customer. They can grab any combination of customer, product, and sales territory to understand growth, mix, and trend within that microcosm.

The measurable impact of this navigational speed is significant. According to Glaxo Wellcome, business reviews for customers or within management that used to take a week now take an hour or part of a morning. Substantial savings in a ubiquitous task like business reviews adds up to weeks of additional selling time per year — for every salesperson in the organization.

Multidimensional managers in sales at Witco Corporation, a $2 billion manufacturer of chemical and petroleum products, now perform *Sales Analysis* in a fraction of the time and they get *more value* from the information. They are continually discovering growth patterns and trends that they could never see before.

Multidimensional sales representatives with *Sales Analysis* are now properly equipped for face-to-face, fact-based selling with customers. Fellowes Manufacturing, the $300 million manufacturer of office supplies, is a leader in this area. Fellowes leverages its own information about the buying patterns of office supply chains to increase Fellowes' value to its customers. On their laptops, Fellowes' sales force can benchmark a customer's mix against the average for all Fellowes' customers. If, in the benchmark, one product is leveraging more sales of a secondary product than is currently the case for the customer, the customer has a clear opportunity to increase business in the secondary product.

In a sense, Fellowes is no longer just selling office supplies to its customers. It is selling information as well. Fellowes has strengthened its position in the market by supplying strategic information to its customers.

Sales Analysis is the primary sweet spot for mastering information in the sales force. It aligns the sales organization around a consistent picture of the business. And it creates a foundation for Way 7.

Way 7 — Customer & Product Profitability

"Today, our salespeople can see their profitability levels by product, by customer, and by market. Before, they weren't sure what their profit levels were and could only focus on sales volume and selling price. Now, they are paying close attention to the product mix and customer type, which maximizes profitability in every sales situation."

— *Domtar Inc.*

Way 7 represents a major step forward in the move to *customer-* and *profit-centric* business models. It creates the distinction between the *revenue* dollars and *gross profit* dollars generated in any sales transaction. It empowers the sales force to make pricing and sales closure decisions based on the direct profit contribution of the sale of any product to any customer. The sales department can micro-manage sales situations with direct knowledge of the impact on the bottom line.

Any expense that can be associated with a transaction leads toward true profitability analysis. Discounts are often the first step because they are easiest to capture. Discounts are recorded on the same invoice as revenue and units, so it is almost no work to add them to *Sales Analysis*. Discounts cut deeply into profitability, especially in the packaged goods industry. H.J. Heinz Company of Canada uses *Sales Analysis* with discounts to analyze first-level profitability with its major customers.

WAY 7

CUSTOMER REVIEW Trenton Automotive, Detroit – Sept. 30/96				
Gross Profit $000s				Layer 4 of 4
	Q1	Q2	Q3	YTD
3/4" Plate	14.1		−20.1	−6.0
1/2" Plate	8.5	35.7	8.5	52.7
3/4" Rolled	−5.3	2.6		−2.7
TOTAL	17.3	38.3	−11.6	44.0

Negative transactions are driving gross margin down at least 15 points at Trenton Automotive so far this year.

The next level of profitability beyond discount is gross margin. This represents the most significant shift from a *revenue-centric* view of sales to a *profit-centric* view. This sweet spot results from adding a single new indicator — the standard product cost — to the classic *Sales Analysis* example. We already know the revenue, so given cost, we can calculate the gross profit and gross profit percent of every transaction.

In reality, deriving this cost in many companies can be extremely difficult. Manufacturing corporations, however, have an unfair advantage. They already have a standard product cost for everything they manufacture. The standard product cost multiplied by the number of units in the transaction captures most of the cost of the transaction. (The only wrinkle is that the standard product cost has to be *accurate*. This is not a trivial issue. In fact, it is critical to profitability, and is addressed in Chapter 7.)

York International takes the discipline of profitability even further. Now that its operating divisions can measure profitability at the sales level, York actually charges the standard product cost to its sales divisions. The divisions then return a contribution arrived at by subtracting each division's operating expenses (including capital charges for use of capital employed) from *gross profit*, instead of from revenue. The divisions are measured on that contribution.

York is one of the first manufacturing companies to achieve full alignment between its sales goals and corporate goals.

Way 8 — Sales Plan vs. Forecast

We can get results to our entire European sales force against daily plan and forecast by 8:30 a.m. after the close of the previous day's business."
— *Fortune 100 Corporation (Consumer Packaged Goods)*

This sweet spot simplifies the most common conversation in sales: "How are we doing against plan?" Behind this simple question are dozens of associated questions that need to be answered before a sales manager has fully absorbed the picture. Are we on plan for the month? Are we on plan for the quarter? Are we on plan YTD? Are each of the people under me on plan? If there is a variance against plan, what's driving it?

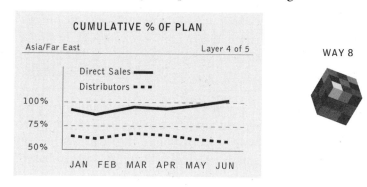

Asia/Far East is off plan but it is distributors, not direct sales, that is driving the variance.

Multidimensional managers answer these questions in minutes. They can see variances visually, then drill down or click through layers to see what is driving each variance. High-level managers can absorb the entire sweep of performance against plan across a large organization in an hour or two, as soon as results are published. Conversations about variances can happen dynamically in meetings, with information in the sweet spot either leading or supporting the direction of the conversation.

In more sophisticated planning organizations, like the Fortune 100 corporation quoted at the beginning of this section, the pay-off isn't just every month. It's daily. "We're delivering up to six plan and forecast lines to our European account teams daily against yesterday's and week-to-date results. Our account teams have to understand their position against plan, rolling forecasts, statistical-driven forecast, and stretch forecast for many accounts and product lines in a few minutes every morning. If we couldn't deliver information packaged for a high absorption rate, we couldn't run the business this way. This planning accuracy is critical for us to drive down costs in the inventory and production process."

Way 9 — Sales Pipeline

"The further we can look ahead to future orders, the more we can make our actuals and our estimates converge — which, for us, is the most efficient point of operation."

— *Maritime Tel & Tel (MT&T)*

This popular sweet spot provides a complete picture of how much is in the pipeline and what is driving it. It organizes the pipeline by geography and by periods into the future. It may also include dimensions such as product, customer, and probability of closing.

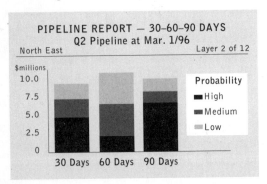

Both the 30-and 90-day forecasts look solid here because most of these forecasts are high-probability business. On the other hand, the 60-day forecast looks soft.

The pipeline process in most manufacturing companies is still relatively primitive. Sales managers canvas their reps by phone for forecasts, then fax or e-mail the forecasts in a spreadsheet to regional managers. At the top, senior management sees a big number by geography and some of the larger pending deals.

Many salesreps, however, now manage their own forecasts in contact databases on their PCs. These contact databases can be uploaded to form a much richer, consolidated picture of the forecast — including specific product forecasts. Packaged and distributed as Way 9, this sweet spot helps production, purchasing, and finance optimize their activities to meet forecast demand.

Way 9 removes the cost penalty for holding the pipeline conversation — the *who* will sell *what* to *whom* by *when* conversation. It simplifies the business review process between sales people and sales management. It increases the reliability of quarterly revenue and income forecasts made by finance to the bank and the investment community. It allows purchasing and production more lead time to adjust inventory and scheduling based on forecasted demand at the product and customer level. By driving actuals and estimates more closely together, it allows the integrated supply chain to optimize its costs.

In Summary

The ultimate goal is to align the sales force with the corporate goal of maximizing profit. The sweet spots in this chapter help achieve this goal in two ways. First, they simplify the most common conversations in sales. What is driving the business? How are we doing against plan? What is in the pipeline? These simple conversations consume weeks of selling and sales management time in the selling year. Eliminating much of this cost *visibly, verifiably, and significantly reduces total overall operating costs.*

Secondly, these sweet spots enable *previously unavailable strategic capabilities*, specifically fact-based selling and the ability to make sales decisions based on customer and product profitability. This latter capability is fundamental to achieving the full profit potential of the business. When the decisions of every member of the sales team are governed by the gross profit impact of their transactions, the sales force is fully aligned with corporate goals.

Way 6 — Sales Analysis

Sales analysis provides "X-ray" vision for determining what is driving the business. It dramatically improves sales force productivity and enables fact-based selling. Note the prepackaged time options for easily tracking growth by year, quarter, or month. Also note the indicators for Discount, the first step on the road to evaluating customer profitability.

TIME PERIODS	ORGANIZATIONS	PRODUCTS	CUSTOMERS	INDICATORS
Years	Sales Divisions	Product Lines	Sales Rank	Ordered Units
Quarters	Sales Districts	Brands	Range	Change Orders
Months	Sales Reps	Products	Top 10	Sold Units
YTD		SKUs	Top 11–100	Revenue
Prior YTD			Etc.	Discount
QTD			Customers	Discount %
Prior QTD				Average Selling Price
Current Month				Inquiries
Prior Month				% Orders to Inquiries
Rolling 12 Months				

Way 7 — Customer & Product Profitability

Customer & Product Profitability is one of the major punchlines in the 24 Ways, transforming the sales force from a revenue-centric to a profit-centric organization. Without Way 7, a sales force lacks the enabling technology to manage product mix and its impact on profitability

TIME PERIODS	ORGANIZATIONS	PRODUCTS	CUSTOMERS	EXCEPTION DIMENSION	INDICATORS
Years	Sales Divisions	Product Lines	Sales Rank	**Gross Profit %**	Units Sold
Quarters	Sales Districts	Brands	Range	**Ranges**	Revenue
Months	Sales Reps	Products	Top 10		Discount%
YTD		SKUs	Top 11–100		Commission %
Prior YTD			Etc.		Material %
QTD			Customers		Shipping %
Prior QTD					Claims %
Current Month					**Gross Profit**
Prior Month					**GP % of Sales**

Sales Plan vs. Forecast simplifies the multi-dimensional conversation that preoccupies sales —who is making their plan, who isn't, and where we are against plan overall.

TIME PERIODS	ORGANIZATIONS	PRODUCTS	% OF PLAN	INDICATORS
This Year	Sales Divisions	Product Lines	> 120%	Plan Units
— —	Sales Districts	Brands	111–120%	Actual Units
4 Quarters	— —	— —	90–99%	Rolling
— —	Sales Reps	Products	<90%	Forecast Units
12 Months				Plan Sales
—				Actual Sales
YTD				**% Plan**
Prior YTD				
QTD				
Prior QTD				
Current Month				
Prior Month				

Way 9 — Sales Pipeline

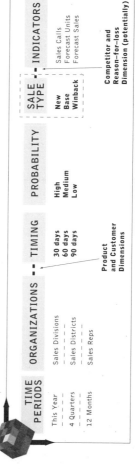

Sales Pipeline information is based on sales force input. The information may already be in popular contact databases such as Act! and GoldMine. Way 9 enables in-depth conversations about pipeline, increases accuracy of corporate forecasts, and quantifies win ratios against key competitors.

TIME PERIODS	ORGANIZATIONS - -	TIMING	PROBABILITY	SALE TYPE -	INDICATORS
This Year	Sales Divisions	30 days	High	**New**	Sales Calls
— —	Sales Districts	60 days	Medium	**Base**	Forecast Units
4 Quarters	— —	90 days	Low	**Winback**	Forecast Sales
— —	Sales Reps				
12 Months		Product and Customer Dimensions		**Competitor and Reason-for-loss Dimension (potentially)**	

Back to the Financial Statements

Income Statement
Revenue ← ❶   WAYS 6–9
  COGS   ← ❷
Gross Profit ← ❷
  SG&A   ❸
Selling ← ❸
  General
  Administration
  Net Profit

Ways 6–9 impact three lines on the income statement. They increase Revenue ❶ through fact-based selling. They increase Gross Profit ❷ by shifting attention from revenue targets to gross-profit targets. They cut down Selling Costs ❸ as a percentage of sales by increasing productivity in the everyday sales process and tightening alignment throughout the sales team.

Chapter 6

In Search of the Ultimate Sweet Spot

"Strategy should be developed from the bottom up, not the top down…In military warfare, the serious student of strategy begins with the study of the bayonet."

— Marketing Warfare, Ries & Trout

Strategy from the Bottom Up

For the serious student of marketing strategy, a top customer isn't a $20 million account. It's a $20 million account with 40 percent gross margin. Strategy from the bottom up in marketing requires this kind of understanding of profitability by customer. You can set profit goals top-down for the company, but they are only realistic if you can see a way to reach those same goals bottom up, one customer at a time.

What marketing discovers about profitability will drive the investment strategies it recommends for product development, geographic channel development, and customer acquisition — all enormous expenditures. The more marketing knows about what profitable customers look like, the lower the investment risk and the higher the likely return.

These investment risks are higher than they should be in most manufacturing corporations today because:

Reason 1. Up to now, marketing has imagined the future more in terms of market share than profit characteristics of its customer portfolio.

Gains in market share are the usual measure of success in marketing. The reason appears clear: market leaders tend to earn strong margins. Yet big gains in market share only happen during relatively short periods of time when a market is created. Over the long term, the strategic issue is how to maximize profitability from the customers you acquire. The question is, how do you acquire customers who will maximize your profitability?

Perhaps understandably, financial institutions have led the way in this portfolio view of the customer. Many leading banks now look at their customers exactly in the same way as they look at an investment portfolio. They analyze the profitability of their accounts. They classify their accounts by profitability tier. They prune out accounts that put downward pressure on overall margins, or manage them up to higher profitability tiers. As yet, most other corporations haven't followed suit.

Reason 2. A bottom-up picture of profitability is difficult to assemble.

The standard marketing view of profitability tends to reflect finance's view, which as we have noted, lacks the customer dimension. At considerable cost, marketing may assemble a profitability report on a specific customer. But there's no easy way to sweep rapidly across the entire customer portfolio — to classify customers by their level of profitability, to identify which characteristics define customers in the higher levels, to understand if the corporation is gaining customers in higher levels or losing them. Without a good bottom-up picture of profitability, it is impossible to build a powerful marketing strategy to acquire the right customers for the future.

Reason 3. In targeting potential customers, profitability is not a key criteria. Marketers don't evaluate the profit potential of customer acquisition programs.

Maximizing response rates and minimizing cost per response is obviously key to operating a direct marketing firm. In general, manufacturing companies don't apply the same level of analysis to their own marketing campaigns. Certainly, they don't evaluate their campaigns against the criterion of high-profit profiles. As a result, manufacturing companies don't get maximum return on their marketing investment. And they don't know whether or not they are acquiring the right customers for an ideal portfolio in the future.

The ideal information sweet spot would identify a portfolio of customers who create maximum profit for the business as it goes forward. Marketing's responsibility is to find that sweet spot and recommend the most cost-effective way to arrive there — a tough proposition if marketing can't put its finger on the pulse of profitability in the business as it stands right now.

Designing a Portfolio of Ideal Customers

There are three ways to increase the proportion of high-profit customers in the portfolio: you can identify and cull out negative contributors; improve the profit contribution of existing customers, so they more closely conform to the ideal profile; or acquire new high-profit customers.

But there is one significant wrinkle in an otherwise straight-forward exercise. The ultimate sweet spot in the future is a moving target. The market, the products, and the competitive environment are continually changing. Reality keeps challenging a marketing strategy with unexpected results and surprises, requiring a process of dynamic adjustment.

Sometimes, these dynamic adjustments cut to the heart of the business. As Peter Drucker pointed out in "The Theory of the Business," another of his classic Harvard Business Review articles, unexpected surprises are often indicators that the "theory of the business," the basic premise of the business held by management at the time, is fundamentally changing. These surprises occur first at a level not usually available in management reports. They appear as subtle shifts in customer profitability, in product mix that may only appear within certain locations, within certain distribution channels, or with certain customer divisions. Unobserved, these surprises are missed opportunities to exploit cash-rich business. These shifts — that may even impact the assumptions of the business — continually alter the latitude and longitude of the ultimate sweet spot.

The information sweet spots in this chapter capture the profitability profile of the existing customer asset, as well as allow for bottom-up strategy building and early adjustment to unexpected successes and failures. The companies noted here — Domtar, Epson America, Moen, and Tropitone — have empowered themselves in the art of dynamic adjustment by constantly tracking the pulse of profitability at strategic points in the business. These companies use innovative dimensions to clarify the source of profitability and refine the focus of the ultimate sweet spot. They build tactical and strategic responses to the evolving market based on *bottom-up* trends at the customer level. As you will soon see, they have learned to focus their marketing investment on building the strongest possible portfolio of profitable customers.

Way 10 — Strategic Marketing Analysis

"By gaining stronger visibility for product margins, we could rationalize our product lines and concentrate on our more profitable grades. We could pick and choose the best products to sell and decide which mills to keep running. In 12 months, we've enormously improved our ability to choose what we want to sell to whom."

— *Domtar*

Strategic Marketing Analysis organizes customers from most valuable to least valuable, charts their lifetime value to date, and captures the number of customers in each profitability tier so the trend in profitability mix can be seen easily over time.

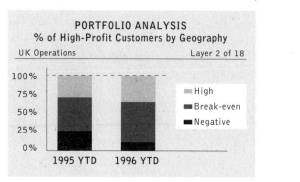

PORTFOLIO ANALYSIS
% of High-Profit Customers by Geography

UK Operations   Layer 2 of 18

WAY 10

- High
- Break-even
- Negative

1995 YTD   1996 YTD

UK Operations has reduced negative-margin contributors as a percentage of total customers over the last year, increasing the overall percentage of high-margin customers.

How does this new perspective influence behavior? Some corporations now consider low-margin customers almost as a separate business unit, applying dedicated management either to return them to profitability or design them out of the business. Another innovative behavior is the practice of regular acquisition and erosion reporting — so senior management is constantly in touch with what's driving the inflow and outflow of customers in high-profitability tiers.

Multidimensional managers in marketing can compare the profitability mix of their customers by geography, by industry, by volume of business, by the number of different products they buy, and by any number of other characteristics. Epson America identifies the profitability characteristics of its customer segments and works on increasing the profitability of each segment. Adding its own dimensional variations to the *Strategic Marketing Analysis* sweet spot, Epson segments its business by warranty type and repair type to find the best ways to increase the profitability of each segment.

Variation on Way 10

"For the first time, we can see which combinations of color, quality, type, or package size are driving customer demand."

— *Unifi, Inc.*

Often, manufacturing companies can't see the impact across the business of important information about products such as color, scent, salt content, and so on — information that clearly impacts sales. The historical design of most information systems embeds these product "attributes" right in the product code, in order to identify each product. As a result, you can get reports on specific products — such as *white* plastic serving spoon number SPWP0000 and *red* plastic serving spoon number SPRP0000 — but you can't see, in general, the popularity of white versus red across all plastic serving utensils, or across all kitchenware, or across the entire business.

Tropitone Inc., an Irvine, California manufacturer of outdoor furniture, was one of the first customers to break out these product "attributes" as full-fledged dimensions in PowerPlay. Suddenly, Tropitone could see the full impact on sales of the color of the furniture, the material of construction (wood, aluminum, plastic) and the combination of both. This knowledge had profound impact on production and inventory planning, with a corresponding impact on profitability.

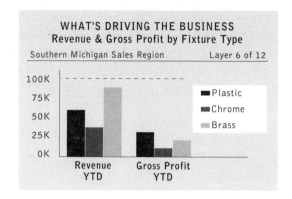

WHAT'S DRIVING THE BUSINESS
Revenue & Gross Profit by Fixture Type

Southern Michigan Sales Region   Layer 6 of 12

WAY 10
VARIATION

Capturing the pulse of profitability from the bottom up — at the product feature level.

Moen Incorporated, a $600 million manufacturer of faucets and plumbing supplies, has also profited from applying Way 10. Moen has untangled a complex product hierarchy into independent dimensions such as product line, finish (i.e. chrome, brass), and handle type. Moen has further mapped these attributes by customer, channel, and organizational responsibility. Now Moen can instantly see which products and customers are driving sales and profitability in each of its markets.

Way 11 — Tactical Marketing Analysis

"We were able to identify our most efficient target customers through direct mail campaign analysis. By targeting our customers better, we can now predict most return rates within 5 percent of forecast."

— *Avon Canada*

Way 11, *Tactical Marketing Analysis*, evaluates the effectiveness of marketing campaigns. Some manufacturers already have sophisticated systems to track incoming leads and record all leads that successfully close. These companies are the exception — but if they have the systems, so much the better. They can use Way 11 to do a *cost per close* analysis rivaling professional direct marketing firms.

The majority of companies who don't yet have these systems can still be in play with *Tactical Marketing Analysis* — as long as they can at least capture the *responses* to their marketing campaigns. *Cost per response* and *percentage response* are not as powerful a set of indicators as *cost per close* and *percentage close*. But marketing can usually capture and manage *responses* within its own resources. And *responses* are a reasonable first approximation in evaluating marketing investment.

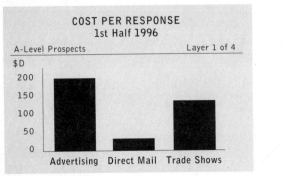

WAY 11

Direct mail was clearly a more cost-effective way to initiate responses from "A-level" prospects in the first half of the year.

Multidimensional managers using this sweet spot have a factual basis for evaluating both the media and the message. They can compare *cost per response* between advertising, direct mail, and trade shows. They can compare different messages in the same medium or test the impact of their messages in different parts of the country by industry type, or by title of the buyers they are targeting. And they can compare the profile of response against the ideal profile of high-profit customers — the right customers for the future.

In Summary

Companies such as Domtar, Epson, Moen, and Tropitone are leading the way in developing marketing strategies from the bottom up. They understand the profit profile of their customers now, so they understand the profile of the most desirable customer in the future. They monitor their inflows and outflows of customers in terms of acquiring or losing strong cash contributors. They concentrate on making each customer more profitable. They have *radically improved productivity in the critical success factor of managing their customer portfolio for maximum return*.

We are assuming, of course, that the profit equation as read by marketing is correct and that the right work is being done in purchasing, the plant, and customer service to maintain or adjust standard product costs to report profitability accurately. More about that in succeeding chapters.

But given that the profitability equation is correct as reported, the company can now link its investments in customer relationships specifically to the returns those customers generate. Marketing can line up the efforts of the entire organization to assemble the sweet spot of customers who should generate the most profit in the future.

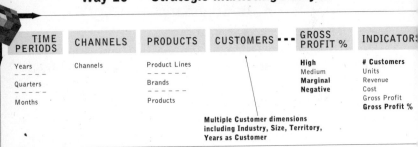

Way 10 — Strategic Marketing Analysis

TIME PERIODS	CHANNELS	PRODUCTS	CUSTOMERS - - -	GROSS PROFIT %	INDICATORS
Years	Channels	Product Lines		**High**	**# Customers**
- - - - -		- - - - -		Medium	Units
Quarters		Brands		**Marginal**	Revenue
- - - - -		- - - - -		**Negative**	Cost
Months		Products			Gross Profit
					Gross Profit %

Multiple Customer dimensions including Industry, Size, Territory, Years as Customer

In this sweet spot, multidimensional managers in marketing track high-profit and low-profit groups of customers. The characteristics of high-profit customers should drive investment in future customer acquisition.

Way 10 Variation

TIME PERIODS	ORGANIZATIONS	OUTDOOR PRODUCTS	COLOR	MATERIAL	INDICATORS
Years	Sales Divisions	Tables	**White**	**Wood**	Revenue
- - - - -	- - - - -	Chairs	**Hot Pink**	**Aluminum**	Units
Quarters	Sales Districts	Lounges	**Salmon**	**Plastic**	Returns
- - - - -	- - - - -		**Beige**		Etc.
Month	Sales Reps				
YTD					
Prior YTD					

This sweet spot is a classic example of elevating product attributes to the level of dimensions. For Tropitone Inc., an outdoor furniture manufacturer, it reveals which colors and materials are driving the business — saving money in production, inventory, and shipping.

Way 11 — Tactical Marketing Analysis

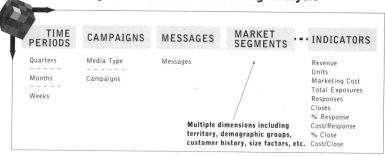

TIME PERIODS	CAMPAIGNS	MESSAGES	MARKET SEGMENTS	••• INDICATORS
Quarters	Media Type	Messages		Revenue
– – – –	– – – – – –			Units
Months	Campaigns			Marketing Cost
– – – –				Total Exposures
Weeks				Responses
				Closes
				% Response
			Multiple dimensions including	Cost/Response
			territory, demographic groups,	% Close
			customer history, size factors, etc.	Cost/Close

This sweet spot is an instant decision support system for evaluating the return on individual campaigns, types of media, mailing lists, and messages. The inflow of acquired customers can be compared against the profile of existing high-profit customers.

Back to the Financial Statements

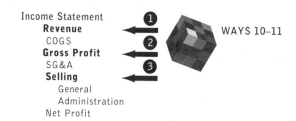

Income Statement
 Revenue ❶
  COGS
 Gross Profit ❷
  SG&A
 Selling ❸
   General
   Administration
  Net Profit

WAYS 10–11

Ways 10–11 impact three lines on the Income statement. They drive Revenue ❶ by isolating what combinations of product mix and customer segments are driving growth. They increase Gross Profit ❷ by targeting prospects with the greatest profit potential. They lower Selling ❸ costs as a percentage of sales by increasing the ROI on promotion dollars.

Chapter 7

Freeing up the Most Cash Fastest

"The line between order and disorder lies in logistics."
— *Sun-Tzu, The Art of Warfare*

"Geese survive; buffalo perish… Hardworking, hard-driving managers get outmaneuvered by more nimble competition."
— *Blasco and Stayer, Flight of the Buffalo*

Purchasing's Leverage on Cash

The purchasing department has unique leverage on a corporation's cash position, particularly through its command over the materials line in the income statement. In many instances, raw materials represent the largest single expense on the income statement. In these cases, the cost of materials drives pricing and the entire cost model of the business. Purchasing negotiations obviously are critical to profitability. Any reductions in the cost of materials drop right into net profit, and strengthen the company's position as a low-cost producer.

Purchasing has a second point of leverage — its influence over inventory levels. This influence may be direct (if purchasing manages inventory itself), or indirect (through the management of reliable delivery by suppliers). If inventory can be reduced, corresponding amounts of cash free up on the balance sheet, and can be reinvested to drive growth.

So purchasing occupies strategic ground in terms of impacting cash flow. At the same time, purchasing has taken on an expanded operational role. Purchasing managers are no longer simply agents; they now manage the entire front end of a tightly integrated supply chain, where performance along the line is critical.

This strategic position of the purchasing department does not translate into maximum impact on cash flow, however, for two specific reasons:

Reason 1. No one can see exactly how much inventory is on hand, where it is, and how fast it is moving.

Purchasing managers don't have a good picture of their inventory. They can't easily spot surpluses or duplication of inventory in different storage locations. They have no easy mechanism to anticipate demand. Consequently, they tend to operate in reactive mode, buying when they receive a purchase order or at preplanned restocking points. They have limited information to make the best trade-offs in long-term contract versus spot-market decisions.

Reason 2. The negotiating game with suppliers is changing. Purchasing managers don't have the information support to play the new game as professionals.

Price isn't the only big issue in the context of integrated supply chain management. Reliability of delivery is every bit as big. The game here is walking the tightrope. Reduce inventory as much as possible, but *never run out.* Running out has serious consequences. Assembly lines shut down. Capacity utilization falls. Standard product costing flies out of kilter. The resulting downstream production costs may be more significant than paying a premium on upstream materials cost.

The reliability of suppliers is the only thing that keeps the manufacturer from losing his balance. The reliability of suppliers, in turn, is governed by two key criteria: the number of times they are contacted by purchasing, and the quality of the contact. But the cost of getting accurate information regarding late, partial, or rejected shipments is too great to fully support frequent, high-quality contact with suppliers.

Cranking Up the Leverage in Purchasing

The principle activities to leverage in purchasing are *managing inventory* and *dealing with suppliers*. In both cases, the *limiting step* is the information-gathering step. In managing inventory, the limiting step is the time taken to find out where surpluses exist in inventory and the rate of *turnover*. In dealing with suppliers, the limiting step is the time taken to gather information to support buying decisions and to monitor the performance of suppliers at the front end of the supply chain. The more nimble purchasing managers can be in assembling this information and bringing it to bear at the critical moment, the greater the potential impact on net profit and cash flow.

The sweet spots in this chapter dramatically increase the speed of information gathering. They also leverage the activity by bringing more comparative information to bear in buying negotiations and in performance management. In buying negotiations, for example, purchasing managers can put reliability on the table equally with price — supported by detailed scoring of the supplier's performance worldwide with comparative scorecards of competitor suppliers. This new information forces quality assurance *upstream* in the supply chain — at its lowest-cost stage in production. As supplier quality improves, the manufacturer saves costs in incoming inspection, and rejections of defective material at higher-cost stages of production. The net result is to add value to the material being acquired at the purchase price, while lowering overall transaction costs across the supply chain.

Similarly, in supplier management, with quickly prepared scorecards evaluating on-time shipment and reliability, each purchasing manager can afford to keep more suppliers at A-level performance. Greater reliability from more suppliers lowers inventory levels, freeing up more cash on the balance sheet.

In manufacturing companies, multiple materials from multiple suppliers are being delivered to multiple plants with varying degrees of success every day. When this complicated picture is simplified — when the activity of *managing inventory* and *dealing with suppliers* is supported with the right information — the impact on the balance sheet can be striking.

Way 12 — Inventory Turnover

"Within 12 months, we shrank the oil inventory we were carrying by nearly 25 percent, freeing up about $500 million in working capital on the balance sheet."

— *Chevron Products*

The lesson Chevron learned was that you don't need much data to have a big impact on your financial statements. In Chevron's case, the amount of data was a 15 MB sweet spot delivered to 60 inventory managers across the company. The information was refreshed weekly. The impact on Chevron's inventory within a year was remarkable — enough to rate an article in Forbes *ASAP* Magazine.

Yet more remarkable was Chevron's time to result. Within two weeks, Chevron had set up its first sweet spot for testing with their inventory managers. Within 30 days, Chevron was seeing the first impact on inventory levels.

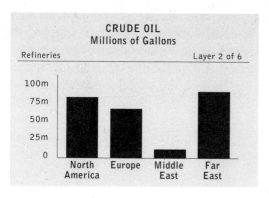

WAY 12

From any starting report, purchasing managers can quickly discover where inventory is located and how fast it is moving.

Inventory Turnover shows purchasing and other inventory managers what inventory they have, where the inventory is held, and how fast it is moving. Surplus inventory anywhere in the system stands out. Rather than purchasing additional inventory if prices are currently high, purchasing managers can substitute surplus inventory from other locations.

With a dynamic picture of inventory usage, buyers can cover more ground and bring greater leverage to the decisive trade-offs — contract versus spot purchases, high-volume versus low-volume purchases — that shave critical percentage points off the cost of goods sold.

Way 13 — Supplier Scorecard

"Within 90 days, we were able to more effectively negotiate and communicate with our suppliers based on a clearer picture of reality."

— *Analog Devices*

The principle activity of purchasing managers used to be buying. Now, it is managing — as manufacturing companies integrate themselves more closely with their suppliers to reduce cost.

With suppliers appearing directly on the assembly line floor, cost may go down, but exposure increases. Who manages these suppliers as the load across the total supply chain shifts to the front? Purchasing managers suddenly have operational responsibility to manage large supplier organizations directly under their control. In this new role, monitoring supplier performance is a highly leveraged activity.

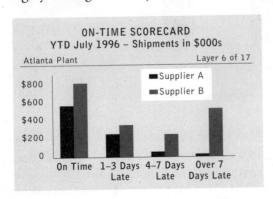

WAY 13

Reducing the steps and time needed to evaluate suppliers increases purchasing managers' leverage in negotiating price and reliability.

Supplier Scorecard is a global picture of the corporation's major suppliers and their performance at all receiving locations. Purchasing managers can evaluate suppliers at any instant, or track their performance over time. They can compare any one supplier's performance with any other's. The time required to prepare these scorecards shrinks from "man-days to minutes." Increasing the productivity of this key managing activity has highly leveraged results: price negotiations that take reliability, comparative price, and the reliability of competitors fully into account.

In Summary

Due to their strategic position in the supply chain, purchasing managers often have more potential to free up cash for operations than other management team members.

The sweet spots in this chapter reduce the time that purchasing managers spend gathering information in two critical areas — inventory levels and supplier performance. Purchasing managers can only maintain inventory at optimum levels if they can see it constantly. They can only negotiate the best price against the trade-off of reliable delivery if they can evaluate suppliers instantly.

By simplifying and speeding these activities, the sweet spots in this chapter *visibly, verifiably, and significantly reduce current total overall operating costs*. The corporation operates with less inventory on hand, fewer downstream production costs caused by poor supplier performance, and materials costs that are either lower or at least include reliable delivery in the price. The productivity increase in purchasing will be reflected in the corporation's cash position and its competitive position as a low-cost producer.

Here, purchasing managers can see where inventory is held and how fast it is moving. As a result, they can anticipate demand, cut the most advantageous contracts, and keep a minimum of inventory on hand.

With Way 13, multi-dimensional managers can compare the performance of suppliers against each other at any location in seconds. Fast supplier evaluation is critical for high-quality and optimized costs at the front end of the supply chain.

Way 12 — Inventory Turnover

TIME PERIODS	INVENTORY	LOCATIONS	PRODUCTS	MATERIALS	T/O RANGE	INDICATORS
Years	Categories	Country	Products		>20	Units
— —	Committed	— —			11–20	Weight
Quarters	Available	Region			6–10	Inv. Cost
— —		Location			1–5	Rolling Average
Months		Warehouse			<1	Units Sold
		Plant				Rolling Average
						Sales
						Inventory Turnover

Multiple dimensions including grades, sizes used in raw material purchases, and restocking.

Way 13 — Supplier Scorecard

TIME PERIODS	SUPPLIERS	MATERIALS	OPERATIONS	TERMS	JUST-IN-TIME PERFORMANCE	INDICATORS
Years	Suppliers	Materials	Region	FOB	Early	# of PO lines
— —			— —	CIF	On time	$ Value
Quarters			Plant		Late	**Lead Time (days)**
— —			— —		Not JIT	**Average Lead Time**
Months			Warehouse			**% Accepted**
						% Complete
						% On time
						% 1–2 days Late
						% 3–7 days Late
						% > 8 days Late

Back to the Financial Statements

Income Statement
Revenue
  Cost of Goods Sold
    Materials
    Conversion
    Shipping
  Gross Profit

WAYS 12–13

Cash Flow Statement
  Sources of Cash
    Net Profit
    Change in Working Capital

Ways 12–13 impact three lines on the income statement. They reduce Materials ❶ as a percentage of revenue by strengthening the negotiating position of buyers. They lower Conversion ❷ as a percentage of revenue by improving supplier performance and therefore reducing supplier-related problems in the plants. They increase Working Capital ❸ by reducing inventory on hand to free up cash.

Chapter 8

Winning in the Plant

"Realize that manufacturing/operations is the prime source of: (1) superior quality, (2) day-to-day product/service innovation, and (3) responsiveness/lead time shortening...Turn manufacturing into a marketing weapon."

— *Tom Peters, Thriving on Chaos*

Breakdowns in the Process

Turning manufacturing into a competitive weapon is a tough assignment. You have to continually find new ways to shorten lead times. You have to increase output per plant to get the maximum return on assets for the people who care about the balance sheet. You have to continually drive production costs down to lead in the pricing game without sacrificing acceptable quality.

This is a world of incremental gains and constant innovations in process that have big impact over the long haul. How fast can you make these incremental gains? That depends on how quickly you can discover the opportunities to improve. The faster you can discover problems, the faster you can resolve them.

There is a pivotal relationship between this discovery process and the efficiency of the production process itself. In the absence of an efficient discovery process, three problems arise:

Problem 1. Manufacturing costs are unnecessarily high; innovation is unnecessarily slow.

Breakdowns in process are rampant in manufacturing plants — machine downtime, rejects, rework hours, engineering changes, unnecessarily wasted material. The big breakdowns get lots of visibility. If an assembly line goes down for two weeks, everyone knows about it, and action is taken immediately. Hundreds of other less-obvious breakdowns get no visibility and are never actively pursued. The irony is that every breakdown — or at least a symptom of every breakdown — is tracked. Every time an assembly line stops, someone enters why it stopped and how long it was down. Similarly, every hour reworking a product that wasn't done right the first time, every pound of scrap, every unit rejected by a quality inspection, gets captured in most manufacturing systems. The information is all there. Yet how often is it ever pulled out of the systems and given to production managers in an understandable format?

Problem 2. Production managers don't see how far they're really off their standard product cost.

Every time a machine failure stalls production of razor blades, the cost of producing razor blades goes up. That unnecessary cost was not factored into the calculation of standard product cost for razor blades. Similarly, every piece of unnecessary scrap, every rejected unit, adds to the actual cost, throwing the standard product cost further out of synch with reality. Who sees this? The issue is that no one sees it. Production managers don't see these kinds of costs at the product level. As a result, they don't see how far they're really off their standard product cost. Neither does anyone else in the company. Meanwhile, sales and marketing managers are making business decisions based on the standard product cost. If the standard product cost is incorrect, their assumptions about profitability are incorrect, too.

Problem 3. Production managers don't understand the *reasons* behind many chronic problems, and therefore can't eliminate them.

Even though the reason for every breakdown is faithfully recorded in many manufacturing operations, the real reasons driving chronic problems elude production managers. Look at the information presented to production managers on equipment failure and you begin to see why. A typical plant contains hundreds of pieces of equipment and dozens of reasons why equipment might fail. Over several plants in a year's production, there may be several thousand instances of equipment failure, causing delays anywhere from a minute to a week. The document that chronicles these several thousand instances defies analysis. The potential gain from isolating the cause of the breakdown may be great — but the price to identify the cause is too high.

Mastering the Discovery Process

The sweet spots in this chapter increase the rate of discovering problems in production. In doing so, they speed innovation — which continually lowers production costs. Resolving a problem in a plant usually has a multiplier effect. If it is associated with a process, it has repeating pay-off over time. Of course, a process breakthrough in one plant can be leveraged in every other plant.

There's another outcome as well, as Hamilton Beach/Proctor-Silex discovered when it cut weeks off customer response lead time. The manufacturer with the shortest lead times gets the business, retains its customers, and can often charge a premium. This is what Tom Peters meant by turning manufacturing into a marketing weapon. This is winning in the plant.

The insight here is that a direct relationship exists between the rate of discovering problems, the rate of innovation in production, and the effectiveness of manufacturing as a marketing weapon. Hundreds of manufacturers like Hamilton Beach/Proctor-Silex, Coors Brewing, Analog Devices, and The Budd Company have used the sweet spots in this chapter to reengineer the process by which production managers discover and resolve problems in their plant.

The faster the discovery process, the fewer the breakdowns. The fewer the breakdowns, the lower the cost of production, the shorter the lead time, and the more positive the impact on the market.

Way 14 — Capacity Management

"We were able to categorize our shippable and gross backlog by age, thereby achieving our customer service objective of reducing delinquent backlog by 100 percent per quarter."

— *Analog Devices*

The first sweet spot for production, *Capacity Management*, captures overall throughput in any one plant, or globally across all plants. It reveals scheduling problems and opportunities at the tactical level. At the strategic level, it is a fundamental tool to maximize return on assets on the balance sheet. With *Capacity Management*, multidimensional managers can instantly see if they are operating at planned capacity, how successfully they are matching capacity to demand, where the bottlenecks are, and what exactly is making up their backlog.

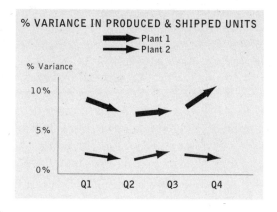

% VARIANCE IN PRODUCED & SHIPPED UNITS

WAY 14

In this example, Plant 1 is shipping about 10 percent fewer units than it produces. Plant 2 is doing a better job in terms of real utilization.

Utilization itself is often overstated when the base indicator is *produced* units. In that case, the utilization rates are only accurate if the plant ships 100 percent of the units it produces. Typically, that doesn't happen because some units are rejected and have to be remanufactured. Therefore, more units are produced than actually shipped because some units have to be produced twice (or more). *Capacity Management* allows production managers and senior management to make the distinction easily.

Backlog, as an indicator, also achieves greater leverage in *Capacity Management.* Usually production managers know where production is bottlenecked, yet they frequently can't quantify the associated backlog accurately. They also can't separate *current* backlog, that is, orders generated in the current period, from *chronic* backlog — unfulfilled orders carried over from previous periods. Chronic backlogs are the orders most at risk for late delivery. They may already be late. When production managers can't separate chronic backlog, they can't manage lead time for the customers who are most exposed.

Way 15 — Standard Product Cost & Quality

"A faster and better understanding of quality issues enabled us to identify which production processes were responsible for low quality."

— *Coors Brewing Co.*

Standard Product Cost & Quality is the primary monitoring station for reject rates, numbers of engineering changes, minutes or hours of production line downtime, pounds of scrap, and hours spent reworking things. For one well-known manufacturer of razor blades, quality is so important that multidimensional managers analyze their razor-blade reject rates on production runs *hourly* with Way 15.

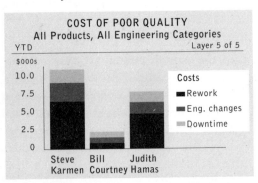

WAY 15

Internal benchmarking points out potentially poor project management skills on the part of Steve Karmen in this example, or potentially important process breakthroughs discovered by Bill Courtney.

Every dimension in *Standard Product Cost & Quality* becomes a benchmark for comparing problem rates. Production managers can compare one plant against another, one assembly line against another, one product line against another, one manager against another. These internal benchmarks increase the rate of discovering problems and successful innovations in business process.

Standard Product Cost & Quality not only reveals problem rates, it captures the costs associated with quality problems and groups them by any dimension — including product.

Production managers can now view the build-up of unnecessary costs by product, and monitor how these unnecessary costs impact their goal of manufacturing at *standard* product cost.

Strategically, this is an important step in the company's ability to adopt a *profit-centric* business model. Without this knowledge in production managers' hands, an unknown and unreported gap exists between the standard cost — on which all the profitability assumptions in chapters 3, 4, and 5 are based — and the actual cost of production. When production managers capture these costs and either eliminate them or include them in future planning, all the basic profit assumptions of the business increase in credibility.

Way 16 — Cause of Poor Quality

"By identifying the sources of defects in minutes versus weeks, we shortened our response time to customers."

— *Hamilton Beach/Proctor-Silex*

Every time an assembly line shuts down, someone on the shop floor notes the date and time and indicates a reason for the delay. It might be out-of-stock material, an incorrect drawing, a bad command-and-control program that runs the machine, poor assembly, equipment failure, or any of a host of other things. This shop-floor entry is added to a list of thousands of similar entries.

Using this list to find the *dominant* reasons driving breakdowns is a frustrating and inefficient process, particularly when you don't know at the outset where to focus your investigation. As a result, the investigation rarely happens and production managers fail to identify and eliminate the cause of many chronic problems.

Cause of Poor Quality presents information in a format that automatically brings attention to dominant reasons. Instead of listing every problem incident, *Cause of Poor Quality* counts the number of incidents by reason and presents the summaries in a highly explorable sweet spot. Production managers can instantly see *which reasons* predominate for any type of breakdown. They can slice and dice their reason counts to see if they are related to specific products, vendors, pieces of equipment, operators, or a multitude of other factors.

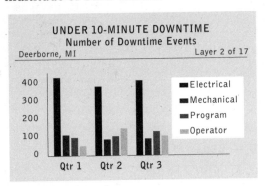

WAY 16

Electrical failure is clearly the root cause of under-10-minute downtime.

The Budd Company, a large manufacturer and supplier of metal stampings and other components for the automotive industry, was one of the first manufacturers to discover the power of Way 15. Budd's issue was downtime. In the automotive business, margins rely heavily on the ability to optimize the production process to accommodate fixed-price contracts. Any time lost due to equipment downtime meant lower margins and threatened Budd's ability to meet just-in-time delivery schedules for customers. Budd needed to know what types of equipment failures occurred, why they occurred, how often equipment was likely to fail, and what happened to equipment after a repair was done.

Budd has now built *Cause of Poor Quality* into its standard production process — analyzing past equipment failures and predicting future failures more accurately than vendor specifications. By mastering this discovery process, Budd has reduced loss of efficiency from equipment breakdowns, shortened lead times, and increased its ability to accommodate just-in-time delivery requirements.

In Summary

The sweet spots in this chapter increase the rate of *discovering problems* and their causes, which is a highly leveraged activity in production. As companies such as Hamilton Beach/Proctor-Silex and The Budd Company have discovered, they *radically improve productivity in two well-understood critical success factors:* quality and lead time.

The speed of problem identification drives the rate of innovation in manufacturing. By increasing the rate of quality improvement, cost reduction, and lead times, these sweet spots enable a dramatic competitive advantage in production, which is an area of prime operational focus for manufacturers. When you're solving production problems faster than your competition, you can ship faster and price lower — turning manufacturing into a marketing weapon.

Way 14 — Capacity Management

Winning in the plant is measured in capacity utilization and yield. Way 14 provides high-speed analysis of real output versus production standards. The exception dimension — Percentage Utilization — immediately isolates all instances of high or low utilization at specific work flow points in the manufacturing cycle.

TIME PERIODS	PRODUCTS	WORK STAGES	PRODUCTION RUNS	UTILIZATION RANGES	INDICATORS
Years	Product Line	Stages	Plants	>100%	Planned Units
Quarters	Brands	Set-up	Runs	91-100%	Produced Units
Months	Products	Assembly		81-90%	Backlog Units
	SKUs	Inspection		<80%	Shipped Units
		Packing			Backlog $
					Shipped $
					Max. Capacity (in Units)
					Utilization
					% Utilization

Way 15 — Standard Product Cost & Quality

Variances between actual product cost and standard product cost are strategically important because they can distort the whole profit picture of the business. Way 15 leads multidimensional managers to the source of the variance.

TIME PERIODS	PRODUCTS	WORK STAGES	PRODUCTION RUNS	INDICATORS
Months	Product Line	Stages	Plants	Planned Units
Weeks	Brands	Set-up	Runs	Production Units
Days	Products	Assembly		Reject Units
	SKUs	Inspection		Rework Units
		Packing		Change Orders
				Uptime
				Downtime
				Std. Product Cost
				Material Cost
				Equipment Cost
				Labor Cost
				Production Cost
				Scrap Cost
				Rework Hours

Way 16 — Cause of Poor Quality

Way 16 slices and dices through hundreds or thousands of problem reports to find the real source of breakdowns. Finding the source of problems faster speeds the rate of cost reduction.

TIME PERIODS	PRODUCTS	WORK STAGES	PRODUCTION RUNS	REASONS	INDICATORS
Years	Product Line	Stages	Plants	**Reasons**	# of QC Problems
– – –	– – –	Set-up	Runs	**Defective**	Downtime
Quarters	Brands	Assembly		**Material**	Std. Product Cost
– – –	– – –	Inspection		**Equipment**	Labor Cost
Months	Products	Packing		**Breakdown**	Production Cost
	– – –			**Operator**	Scrap Cost
	SKUs			**Error**	Rework Hours
				Etc.	Rework Cost

79

Back to the Financial Statements

Income Statement
   Revenue
   COGS
      Materials
      Conversion
   Shipping
   Gross Profit

WAYS 14–16

Ways 14–16 impact three lines on the income statement directly. They increase Revenue ❶ by shortening lead time to customers and strengthening the company's position as a low-cost producer. They lower Conversion ❷ as a percentage of revenue by eliminating costs in the plant and increasing capacity utilization. They increase the accuracy of Gross Profit ❸ as reported in the income statement by aligning actual product cost more closely with standard production cost.

Chapter 9

Solving the Dilemma in the Delivery System

"If something can't be measured, it can't be improved."
— *Jim Harrington, former chairman*
of the American Society for Quality Control

What Got Delivered When

Customers don't draw a line between a manufacturer and the carriers that deliver the manufacturer's product to their receiving docks. If the shipment is late, customers blame the manufacturer. The dilemma for the manufacturer is that there *is* a line, and it is drawn at the end of their shipping docks. Beyond that line — except for the few companies that have sophisticated linked information systems with their customers — the manufacturer's direct knowledge of what is happening ends. For distribution managers, this situation is like working with one hand — or both hands — tied behind their backs.

Problem 1. The goal line for the company is the shipping dock, not the customer.

By default, ship date becomes the measure of success for fulfilling customer requirements, rather than the truly critical measure — date received.

Problem 2. Distribution managers lack negotiating leverage with carriers.

Most distribution managers don't have the facts to effectively benchmark their carriers and therefore force the best combination of performance and price.

Understanding the Dilemma

As noted earlier, the manufacturer's view of the information supply chain typically ends at the shipping docks. The supply chain carries on relentlessly to the customer's receiving dock; the information trail is picked up by the carriers' information system. Note that *carriers* is plural. There are many carriers, all of whom define data in their own ways.

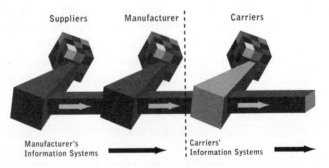

A corporation's view of its supply chain often ends at its shipping docks.

To understand the importance of this break in the information chain, it's worth considering for a moment exactly how the standard shipping process works. When goods leave the manufacturer's shipping dock and are loaded onto a carrier's truck, they are *recorded on the carrier's bill of lading.* This document now becomes the control document in the transaction cycle. The control document is now *out of the manufacturer's hands.*

The recording of important events such as the signing for receipt of goods by the customer is done by the carrier. Rather than detailed information, all the manufacturer typically gets back from the carrier is an invoice covering *all* shipments carried to *all* customers during the period in question. The tracking mechanism for an individual line item on the customer's original order is completely broken.

Furthermore, the customer — who receives the shipment and also records the timeliness of the delivery — typically doesn't capture the manufacturer's tag number or run number. The customer enters the line items from the bill of lading under new codes related to the customer's own production process. So the trail of information is broken here as well.

The ultimate solution is for manufacturers and their customers to link their production systems directly so they can share a common base of information. But that process — electronically linking the production systems of hundreds or thousands of companies — won't happen overnight.

In the meantime, the sweet spot in this chapter will untie at least one hand for distribution managers. Even if the information trail ends at the shipping dock, the manufacturer is still in charge of the consignment *when the goods are released for shipment.* At this point, the manufacturer is still in control of all the particulars — what is shipping, where, how, and at what cost. With this information alone, corporations can generate a powerful new illumination of costs.

Way 17 — Carrier Scorecard

"Our transportation area estimates Way 17 will significantly reduce its total freight costs through improved distribution and transportation processes."

— *Armstrong World Industries*

Way 17 assembles the facts that strengthen distribution managers' negotiating power with carriers. The most important fact is the *distance* between your shipping dock and your major customer locations. Once you know the distance to each customer location, you can calculate the key benchmark — *cost per mile shipped*. Based on the weight of the shipment and the number of units, you can also calculate *cost per ton shipped* and *cost per unit*. Now you have comparative metrics for carrier evaluation — based purely on the information you had when you released the shipment.

These metrics quickly reveal wide variances in *cost per mile* benchmarks. The location of the customer, in particular, typically causes large swings in this benchmark. Like passenger airlines, carriers charge different rates on different routes. But the rates also move dynamically with supply and demand. If one carrier in one location becomes popular, the rates for the popular carrier go up — unless they're pinned down in long-term contracts.

With Way 17, distribution managers have many new options to play the rates. They can push volume to carriers that are least expensive in particular geographical areas. They can negotiate favorable fixed-price contracts in areas where rates are unpredictable.

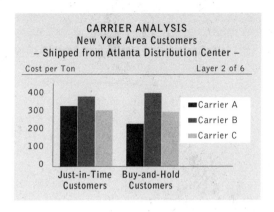

WAY 17

Why are we paying a premium to Carrier B for delivery to buy-and-hold customers? Also, why don't we funnel more business to Carrier A in general?

And there's more to gain. Multidimensional managers in distribution can benchmark carrier types, as well as individual carriers. In other words, they can compare truck, rail, and air carriers across locations. With this knowledge, they can direct business to the right carrier type based on *customer profile.* Way 17 groups customers into two profiles: *just-in-time* customers need shipments urgently; *buy-and-hold* customers typically inventory the shipment and are not as concerned about timely deliveries.

Once they easily distinguish their *buy-and-hold* customers, distribution managers can examine creative options to batch materials into larger or dedicated shipments, which are less expensive — per mile and per ton. They know when they have to pay premium rates and when they can safely cut costs on shipping charges.

Distribution managers work in a volatile market, not unlike traders in the financial market. The comparative benchmarks for negotiation are constantly changing based on global supply and demand. To take maximum advantage of market opportunities, distribution managers must continually shift orders to lower-cost carriers on popular routes, or balance risks of long-term contract versus potential bargains on the spot market.

The limiting factor is the *information gathering* time to support negotiation and rapid action. Way 17 eliminates information gathering as the limiting step in the evaluation and negotiation process. Multidimensional managers in distribution handle more negotiations effectively, maximize more market opportunities, and squeeze costs out of the shipping line in the income statement day after day.

In Summary

Distribution managers often work with both hands tied behind their back. As a rule, they are not well supplied with information. Partially, they are caught in the delivery system's dilemma. The important information about *what got delivered and when* is fragmented in information systems owned by dozens of carriers and hundreds or thousands of customers. In addition, the valuable information that does exist in the corporation is not readily available.

The sweet spot in this chapter unties at least one hand of the distribution manager. Way 17 provides the informational benchmarks that increase the effectiveness of distribution managers in their negotiations with suppliers. In doing so, they *visibly, verifiably, and significantly reduce total operating costs.*

At the same time, when information about delivery times on the customer's receiving dock is not fully available, they can provide reasonable assumptions that start to unwind the dilemma in the delivery system, as we will see in the next chapter. That lays the groundwork to *radically improve productivity in an already well-understood critical success factor* — customer satisfaction.

Way 17 — Carrier Score Card

TIME PERIODS	CARRIERS	DESTINATIONS	CUSTOMERS	DISTANCE FACTOR	CUSTOMER TYPE	INDICATORS
Years	Type	Regions	Segment	Short	Just-in-Time	Trips
– – – –	Truck	– – – –	– – – –	Medium	Buy-and-Hold	Unit
Quarters	Rail	Territories	Customers	Long		Weight Carried
– – – –	Air	– – – –				Distance
Months	Ship	Cities				Cost per Mile/Km
	Combo					Cost per Lb/Kg
						Trips On time
						% On time

Way 17 isolates carrier costs — individually and compared to other carriers — at every customer location. The important benchmarks are cost per unit shipped and the cost per mile (or kilometer) of delivered goods.

Back to the Financial Statements

Income Statement   WAY 17
Revenue
COGS
Materials
Conversion
Shipping ←❶
Gross Profit

Way 17 impacts the Shipping ❶ line on the income statement. It reduces shipping expenses by giving shipping managers the facts to negotiate better deals with their carriers. It also opens the door to other creative strategies that cut distribution cost.

Chapter 10

Customers for Life

"Most businesses lose about 25 percent of their customers annually."
— *Pepper & Rogers, The One to One Future "*

"On average, the CEOs of most U.S. corporations lose half their customers every five years."

— *Frederick F. Reichheld,*
Harvard Business Review, Mar.+Apr. 1996

A Lifetime of Full Profit Potential

In general, the longer a customer stays with a company, the more that customer is worth. In his *Harvard Business Review* article "Learning from Customer Defections," Frederick Reichheld writes, "Long-term customers buy more, take less of a company's time, are less sensitive to price, and bring in new customers. Best of all, they have no acquisition or start-up cost… Good long-standing customers are worth so much that in some industries, reducing customer defections by as little as five points — from, say, 15 percent to 10 percent per year — can *double* profits."

The economics of customer loyalty are driving manufacturing companies — taking the lead from insurance companies — to look at customers like insurance policies. They are starting to calculate the lifetime value of their customer relationships. Losing the lifetime value of a major customer is a serious financial setback. Also, more investment is targeted at increasing business and profitability within these existing customers. But it's difficult to achieve the goals of longer relationships and full profit potential when:

Problem 1. Late shipment information gets little visibility even though it is the *#1 cause of customer dissatisfaction*.

The best way to lose customers is to ship late consistently. Late shipments are a proven barometer of customer dissatisfaction. Amazingly, a track record of delivery history for any customer is difficult to find in most manufacturing companies. For one thing, the information is hard to get, as we explored in the last chapter. But there are ways to at least approximate the current track record with customers and get it in front of as many managers as possible.

Problem 2. The reasons driving most complaints, returns, and claims aren't known.

Complaints, returns, and claims are important opportunities to pursue full profit potential. They are early indicators of serious trouble. Also, studies show that unhappy customers tell their stories to nine other people on average. So the real damage is even worse than it looks. Most manufacturers don't have an efficient way to get these early indicators in front of either senior management or the appropriate customer account teams.

Problem 3. The cost of customer relationships isn't tracked and recaptured in customer pricing.

The cost of servicing customer relationships varies widely. Customers that place high demands on a supplier should be identified so that either the costs can be applied back to products, or special pricing created to cover them.

The fundamental insight in this chapter is that *early* indicators of customer dissatisfaction largely go unexploited. Instead, most companies rely on their mainstream indicators: revenue and growth. But these are *late* indicators. When revenue for an account drops, it indicates more than just dissatisfaction. It indicates that the customer already has built new relationships. It indicates that the full profit potential for that customer is already lost.

The sweet spots in this chapter monitor the *early* indicators — late shipments, complaints, returns, and claims. They quantify a manufacturer's likely exposure, across the full scope of the business and down to the individual account. At the same time, they capture the non-operational costs of the relationship, which may have been missed in calculating the customer's reported profitability.

Getting to the Customer's Receiving Dock

As we discussed in the last chapter, if late shipment is an issue, a manufacturer likely has a serious underlying problem. Most manufacturers lack solid information about when shipments actually reach customer locations. Shipping information resides with carriers and customers, in incompatible systems. Manufacturers lose sight of their shipments at the end of their own shipping docks. To know if customers are happy or not, manufacturers need this detailed delivery information. To get it, they have three options:

Get the information from customers. This is the ideal solution, made easier to some degree by the arrival of the Internet. Nonetheless, sharing information with hundreds or thousands of customers is a daunting task of coordination. It certainly isn't a 90-day project. On the other hand, it is a project that's worth starting, especially with one's largest and most profitable customers — the customers with the greatest lifetime value.

Get the information from carriers. This is a good strategy because delivery information about many customers can come from one carrier. In general, manufacturers should make this a condition of contracts they negotiate with carriers.

Create proxy information. In the absence of accurate information from customers or carriers, manufacturers can arbitrarily create a set of *distance zones* from their warehouses to their customers' locations. Then they can estimate a standard number of days a normal shipment should take by train, truck, and air to get to each zone. Next, they can add this standard number of days to the date on which their production department releases any shipment — based on the zone of the customer's location. The picture developed using this proxy information will not be 100 percent accurate. But at least manufacturers can now report their *estimated* on-time performance. And that's major progress.

Any of these options, or a combination of these options, provides some picture of the action at the customers' receiving docks — and sets up the first sweet spot in this chapter.

Way 18 — On-Time Delivery

"We give late shipment information to everyone who has anything to do with the customer. We give it to everyone on the sales team. We even put it on the shop floor so people in the plant can see the impact they're having on customer deliveries."

— *Ametek/US Gauge*

The first sweet spot measures the prime drivers of customer satisfaction — late shipments and complete shipments. It's difficult to lose a customer when shipments are 100 percent on time and 100 percent complete. With those kinds of marks, a manufacturer can charge a premium.

Like all of the 24 Ways, Way 18 simplifies many multi-dimensional relationships. Multidimensional managers can quickly see performance by overall product line, by individual SKU, by overall geographical area, or by individual customer. They can see which plants are keeping or missing their dates. They can see where performance is getting better and where it's getting worse.

As an instant scorecard, Way 18 is particularly efficient. It includes an "exception dimension," which groups all shipments by how they scored on lateness.

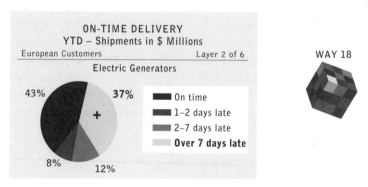

What's driving customer dissatisfaction? The exception dimension in this report shows that 37 percent of Electric Generator shipments to European customers are over seven days late.

In seconds, multidimensional managers can see an on-time delivery scorecard for any product line, plant, or customer. If they are selling a mix of products to any customer, they can quickly see what is driving late shipments across the mix. Managers in different parts of the company can see the same scorecards, size up the situation, and take action to bring deliveries back on track.

This simplicity of evaluating becomes even more important as companies adopt increasingly higher standards for customer satisfaction. A leading Fortune 1000 computer chip manufacturer now measures itself not only against when they *promised* to deliver, but also against the date *requested by the customer*. This higher standard of excellence creates a world that has twice the combinations and therefore twice the complexity. Adopting this higher standard without multidimensional managers to monitor it might not be practical. For such companies, however, the higher standard simply becomes a second "exception dimension" that groups shipments by the *requested* delivery date. The first exception dimension groups the same shipments by the *promised* delivery date. Multidimensional managers can then flip back and forth between dimensions, or compare them side by side.

On-Time Delivery is an important sweet spot to share across the organization. Armed with this information, salespeople can anticipate customer complaints that would otherwise blindside them in sales calls. They also have the facts they need to apply pressure on manufacturing to protect the relationship. At the same time, production managers on the shop floor get direct feedback on the impact that production delays have on customer satisfaction.

Way 18 is the prime "early warning system" of customer dissatisfaction. It has value in at least four departments — and should be shared.

Way 19 — Complaints, Returns, and Claims

"We now have immediate access to product claims information, which enables us to quickly correct manufacturing process defects."
— *Armstrong World Industries*

Beyond late shipments, why are customers unhappy? For big corporations, Way 19 may be the only cost-effective way to find out. Crown, Cork & Seal, a $10 billion manufacturer of plastic and metal containers, is a prime example. The company relies on customer service as a major differentiator. As a point of principle, it carefully tracks all complaints. What Crown, Cork & Seal discovered, however, is that all the detail did not result in greater understanding. In a $10 billion operation, the sheer volume of data across all regions and customers made it literally impossible for the company to put its finger on the most critical complaints.

Here's the point. The complaint process should be a highly efficient form of communication for both parties. After all, individual customers are going out of their way — at some cost to themselves — to spell out the steps to a more positive relationship. But big companies lack a cost-effective way of listening.

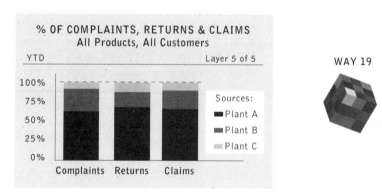

Over 60 percent of the total volume of complaints, returns, and claims are related to production from Plant A.

The answer for Crown, Cork & Seal was Way 19. Crown, Cork & Seal managers could suddenly master the "sheer volume" of data and quickly pick out the most critical customer concerns. They could instantly identify the sources of most complaints. Then they could use a "reason" dimension to find out the cause of the complaint.

The "reason" dimension, in particular, makes Way 19 remarkably effective for understanding large numbers of complaints. Huge numbers of individual returns, claims, or complaints are assigned to a relatively small number of reasons. Often there are fewer than 100 reasons that really make a difference in pinpointing customer concerns. Each reason is like a bucket; each return, claim, or complaint, a drop of water. Instead of focusing on the drops of water as in the past, Crown, Cork & Seal managers can now look at which buckets have the most water.

If the reason for many complaints is "discoloration of material," Crown, Cork & Seal can then instantly bring in other dimensions to find out: what product is responsible, is it in a particular area only, is it coming from one particular plant? Analysis time compresses from "impossible" to "seconds."

Crown, Cork & Seal is now tackling areas of the business it never knew were causing problems with customers.

Way 20 — Cost of Service Relationship

"By gaining a clearer picture of the cause of our customer claims, we were able to assess what the real costs of maintaining customer relationships were."
— *Air Products and Chemicals, Inc.*

If you look at all the activities across a business, some are planned and operate in an "efficient channel." Some aren't planned and operate in an "inefficient channel." Returns, claims, complaints, and change orders are prime examples. They are not in anyone's plan. They chew up salespeople's time, product marketing people's time, production time. They are typically handled on a one-off basis. The ROI is low in the "inefficient channel" for the simple reason that there is little leverage in one-off activities.

Obviously, corporations want to minimize the amount of "inefficient channel" activity, or at least price appropriately to cover it. But before they can minimize it, or price to cover it, they have to identify it. That's the purpose of Way 20.

COST OF SERVICE REVIEW
Customer: RMC Industrial
12 months ending Sept. 30

WAY 20

	Avg. All Customers	RMC Europe	RMC USA
Change orders as % of total orders	3%	10%	7%
$ Returns as % of $ Revenue	2%	8%	5%
Inquiries per Month per order	3.1	12.1	8.4

Both European and North American divisions of RMC Industrial are well over average in cost of servicing the relationship. The relationship with these divisions may not be profitable.

Way 20 tracks "hits" on the organization — initiated by the customer — which drive costs in the "inefficient channel." To calculate the total expense to service these hits would take a full-blown activity-based costing system. That might be worth doing in the long run. With Way 20, however, corporations can get a good relative picture of the activities generated by one customer versus another. Using that picture, multidimensional managers can quickly determine if there are any predominant causes behind the activity. Is it a particular product? A particular sales team? A particular segment of customers? Or do some customers just demand more "inefficient channel" attention?

The answer to these questions leads to two actions. If it is a particular product or sales team, then changes can likely be made to reduce costs in the "inefficient channel" and therefore increase profits. If it's just the nature of certain customers, the relationship can be repriced to cover the extra demands.

In Summary

The lifetime value of a highly profitable customer represents a considerable financial asset. As a result, recognizing *early* indicators of customer dissatisfaction among your best customers is a highly leveraged activity. By providing these *early* indicators, and by increasing the rate at which this critical activity can be performed, the sweet spots in this chapter *radically improve productivity in an already well-understood critical success factor —* increased retention rates for high-profit customers.

Since it is cheaper to conduct business with existing customers, the increase in retention rates *visibly, verifiably, and significantly reduces total operating costs.* Eliminating or repricing high-cost-of-service relationships also reduces total operating costs.

But the manufacturer isn't the only one to gain significant cost reductions from the sweet spots in this chapter. Returns and claims aren't cheap for customers either. They hit the customer's "inefficient channel," spawning non-value-added activities and costs. The manufacturer's late deliveries can jeopardize the customer's ability to deliver reliably, with all kinds of down-stream financial consequences. As these sweet spots kick in, the customers' financial statements strengthen as well.

Way 18 — On-Time Delivery

TIME PERIODS	PRODUCTS	LOCATIONS	CUSTOMERS	DELIVERY LEAD TIMES	%LATE Promised	%LATE Requested	INDICATORS
Years	Product Line	Territories	Segments	>30 Days		**% On time**	$ Value
– – –	– – –	– – –	Customers	6–30 Days		**% 1–2 Days Late**	# PO Lines
Quarters	Brands	Plants		1–5 Days		**% 3–7 Days Late**	# Accepted
– – –	– – –	Warehouses		Same Day		**% >7 Days Late**	% Accepted
Months	Products						# Complete
	SKUs						% Complete

Scorecarding yourself!

For most manufacturing companies, this is the #1 scorecard of customer dissatisfaction. It should be in the hands of senior as well as sales, marketing, customer service, and production managers.

Way 19 — Complaints, Returns, and Claims

TIME PERIODS	PRODUCTS	CUSTOMERS	LOCATIONS	REASONS	INDICATORS
Years	Product Line	Segments	Regions	Order Status	# Inquiries
– – –	– – –	– – –	– – –	Misshipment	# Complaints
Quarters	Brands	Customers	Territories	Defective Parts	**# Returns**
– – –	– – –		– – –	Etc.	**$ Returns**
Months	Products		Cities		**# Claims**
	SKUs				**$ Claims**

Unplanned costs overstate customer profitability

Way 19 is the #2 scorecard of customer dissatisfaction. It highlights breakdowns in quality or other business processes, and captures the reasons stated by the customer. Some companies add exception dimensions for claim severity or response priority to give urgent issues separate consideration.

99

Way 20 — Cost of Service Relationship

TIME PERIODS	PRODUCTS	CUSTOMERS	TERRITORIES	TRANSACTION COMPLEXITY	INDICATORS
Years	Product Line	Segment	Regions	Transactions	Units
– – – –	– – – –	– – – –	– – – –	Standard	Revenue
Quarters	Brands	Customers	Territories	Complex	Cost
– – – –	– – – –		– – – –		Gross Margin
Months	Products		Cities		# Orders
	– – – –				# Special Orders
	SKUs				# Change Orders
					# Inquiries
					# Complaints
					# Returns
					$ Returns
					# Claims
					$ Claims

**Unplanned costs overstate
customer profitability**

*Way 20 quantifies the unplanned costs of customer-driven activities. These costs become the basis of
repricing the relationship to maximize profitability.*

Back to the Financial Statements

Income Statement
    Revenue ← ❶   WAYS 17–20
    COGS ← ❷
    Gross Profit
    SG&A ← ❸
    Net Profit

Ways 18 – 20 impact three lines on the income statement in particular. They increase Revenue ❶ by helping the corporation retain customers. They increase the accuracy of Gross Profit ❷ by highlighting returns that should be charged to standard product costs. They increase Net Profit ❸ by leveraging the cost of the sales force through increased repeat business and by identifying customers who should be charged premiums for high service levels.

Chapter 11

Core Competence in Survival

"Few large corporations live even half as long as a person...The chances are fifty-fifty that readers of this book will see their present firm disappear during their working career."

— *Peter Senge, The Fifth Discipline*

"Some theories of the business are so powerful that they last for a long time. But being human artifacts they don't last forever, and, indeed, today they rarely last for long at all."

— *Peter Drucker, The Theory of the Business*

Staying at the Front of the Evolutionary Curve

Fundamental theories of the business are under constant attack, as Peter Drucker tells us in the article quoted above. To survive, corporations must learn to shift behaviors in their organizations quickly to support new theories and assumptions about the business. Even if the theory of the business remains valid, corporations must continually innovate to remain competitive, finding new behavior patterns that increase profitability per employee.

New behavior patterns require new skills and information

flows. The corporations who learn to introduce these new skills and information flows quickly and successfully develop a core competence in survival. These corporations are constantly identifying and eliminating the skill and information gaps that slow their speed of evolution. Most corporations, however, are unable to gain control over the speed of their organizational evolution for three reasons:

Reason 1. Human Resources information about employee skills or other employee characteristics has limited visibility.

After finance, human resources is the second largest provider of information for internal managers. But HR has few of finance's advantages in this role. It has a tighter budget, no mandate as an information provider, and no supporting cast of analysts on hand. Strategically, HR's task is to drive the skills mix in the company forward at the same rate as the strategic direction of the business. But the skills inventory held in HR is rarely taken seriously and HR, as the owner of this information, remains a background player.

Reason 2. The information that corporations track about their employees is never linked back to financial results.

HR information could *predict output* if it was directly related to the key performance indicators of the business. HR tracks a lot of information that correlates to employee productivity. *Skill* is only one example. What about educational background, years in job, salary level, performance rating? An information source like this about customers or prospects would be a gold mine for marketing managers! This HR information — linked to performance measures — could quantify the impact of skills gaps on the full profit potential of the business. But the link between a corporation's HR information and its financial statements is rarely made. Considering the inseparable relationship between employees and profitability, it is an amazing oversight.

Reason 3. Poor demonstration of ROI on HR and IT strategies slows investment by senior management.

Senior executives recognize that investments in information technology and HR strategies are among the most important decisions they make. But they rarely see clear ROI progress statements to validate or correct their decisions. This reality is partially an outcome of *Reason 2:* the information that corporations track about employees is rarely linked back to financial results. For instance, an upgrade of skills in sales typically isn't tracked against improved cost of sales. As a result, it's never possible to validate which skills are actually *core competencies* that have a material impact on the business. This lack of substantiation creates a climate of uncertainty, stalling investment in strategic initiatives, slowing evolution, and putting the entire business at greater risk.

The fundamental insight in Chapter 11 is that most corporations provide HR information without the punch line. They track the cost of their employees and many of the characteristics of their employees. But they don't connect either of those information sources back to corporate profit.

Closing the loop — where and how does management see a direct return on their human resources strategy?

Typically, senior managers can only monitor high-level indicators of productivity, such as revenue per employee. If revenue per employee goes up, these managers might *suspect* that their human resources strategy was a factor. But how do they know for sure? And how big a factor was it? To find out, they need to combine the cost and skills mix information from the Payroll and HR systems shown in the circles above, with real live operating results.

The Key Partnership

Throughout *The Multidimensional Manager*, each of the 24 Ways is brought to life through a partnership between business managers and the IT professionals who can assemble the right information for them.

In this chapter, the partnership with IT is particularly critical because it breaks new ground. It connects information that typically has never been connected before — the cost and skills mix information from the Payroll and HR systems with performance results from operational systems across the supply chain. The pay-off from the partnership is substantial. Management can see the impact of IT strategies on employee productivity, and judge accurately if high salaries and high skill levels are aligned. Most importantly, it allows general management to validate which employee skills are proven *core competencies* with measurable impact on performance.

The sweet spots in this chapter are a simple, cost-effective way to unlock the real potential of HR information. At the tactical level, they increase the productivity and analysis capability of HR managers without adding layers of additional cost. At the strategic level, they make the connection between the cost of people, the skills mix of the people, and the impact of those two together on profit. If the corporation introduces a new set of skills across its plant, for example, was it worthwhile? Did the introduction of new skills improve results? Now there are Ways to answer these questions.

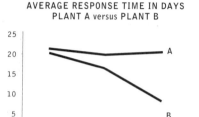

AVERAGE RESPONSE TIME IN DAYS
PLANT A versus PLANT B

Introducing new skills — and relating the impact of HR reengineering directly to primary drivers of revenue and profit.

This new visibility for the impact of HR decisions will change HR's role in corporations. Multidimensional managers in HR will be the first to have new insights into the drivers of employee productivity. They will be the first to "drill down" into the classic productivity indicator — revenue per employee — and find out which employee characteristics are driving that ratio.

At that point, multidimensional managers in HR will be every bit as significant to corporate results as multidimensional managers in other departments who are finding an edge in information about products, carriers, suppliers, markets, and customers. At higher levels in the corporation, senior executives can set targets for the corporation's speed of evolution, and track their progress against plan.

Way 21 — Human Resource Administration

"With the speed of analysis and report creation we can do now, our report turnaround time in HR has gone from weeks to minutes."
— *Compaq Computer Corporation*

The first HR sweet spot captures the company's entire invest-ment in its people. It includes all labor costs and head count company-wide, plus the distribution of those costs across job functions, organizational departments, and salary grades. In rela-tion to the financial statement, it provides substantially greater "drill-down" detail on all salary and labor line items in the income statement.

Way 21 dramatically increases the rate at which HR managers can perform the activity of analysis and report creation. As in finance, before the appearance of multidimensional managers, the HR department functions largely like a production shop, answering similar questions over and over again for operational management. The questions are important — how many employees do we have, what are their functions, how fast are their numbers growing in every part of the company, how quickly are salaries growing — and gathering the information to answer the questions consumes HR's resources.

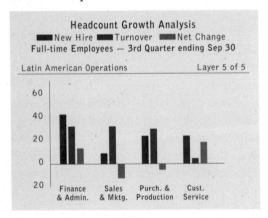

WAY 21

Net change below the line shows that headcount in two revenue-generating departments is decreasing, while net change above the line shows headcount in overhead departments is on the rise.

Way 21 eliminates the time and cost of gathering information to answer these routine questions. Multidimensional managers with Way 21 can quickly report what is driving hiring anywhere in the company, where salaries are increasing fastest, and what is happening to key ratios such as managers to employees, managers to secretaries, and salesreps to service people. Questions that took weeks of turnaround time to answer now take minutes.

In labor negotiations, Way 21 is a strategic advantage, allowing HR managers to see the current position of multiple bargaining groups concurrently, and to calculate instantly the impact of dynamically changing offers and counter-offers.

The productivity of HR managers increases further when HR departments distribute subsets of Way 21 directly to operational managers. Essentially, HR managers can replace the lower-leverage activity of *report creation* with the higher-leverage activity of *information distribution*. Operational managers who receive Way 21 information answer their own questions faster by removing the middleman. And because they are closer to the business, they can often perform more valuable analysis of their own affairs.

Way 22 — Core Competence Inventory

"We can now see strategically exactly what comprises our work force. With manpower information now available on demand, we are able to identify key trends in our employee base. This information helps us to make strategic decisions about work force planning."

— *Compaq Computer Corporation*

A "core competency" is a skill that can have a material impact on the business. The inventory of core competencies captured in Way 22 is a small subset of all skills in the corporation — the sweet spot of skills thought to have a measurable impact on performance. In theory, HR's role is to help define these core competencies and evolve the inventory in line with the direction of the business. In principle, however, skills are never shown to have a material impact on the business, so the skills inventory is rarely taken seriously and the theory never gets practical implementation.

Ways 22, 23, and 24 in combination *confirm the value* of the core competence inventory. These three Ways form the fundamental infrastructure for developing a core competence in survival. Way 22 is step one. It provides a cross-organizational view of skills gaps that are slowing evolution. It tracks progress against plan in spreading new skills that enable new behaviors with potentially higher productivity. It also starts to relate skill levels to compensation. High-end compensation should correspond to high skill level within any job family. The illustration below shows the reverse. The bars show average skill level declining, while the line graph shows average salary going up.

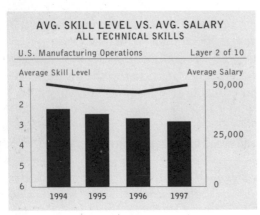

WAY 22

Average skill level is decreasing while average salary increases. Productivity—output per resource unit — in U.S. Manufacturing Operations is going down.

The analysis of core competence versus compensation often reveals the first important insights into maximizing return on investment in employees. Multidimensional managers with Way 22 can line up compensation with core competence to get the most out of the total salary line on the income statement.

Like highly profitable customers, employees with high skill levels in *core competencies* have unusual value to the corporation. Identifying and retaining these employees becomes a key strategy. Multidimensional managers with Way 22 can track retention and growth of these high-value employees. They can also identify employees who lack core competencies, pinpointing likely gaps in full profit potential. They can instantly report the skill mix in any department, develop plans on how that mix should alter, and then track progress against plan.

As each core competency is validated in Way 24, Way 22 becomes increasingly important in management planning. Ultimately, as it proves to be a predictor of the financial plan, it is taken as seriously as the financial plan itself.

Way 23 — BI Deployment

"We measure our rate of adopting certain technologies as a critical success factor in staying competitive. Our rate of creating multidimensional managers tells us how fast we're reengineering our delivery of information across the company and how quickly we're reducing the cost of working with information."

— *Titan Industrial Corporation*

Way 23 is the next step in developing a core competence in survival. It tracks two important new indicators in corporations: the number of Ways deployed, and the number of multidimensional managers across the organization.

For IT departments and general management, these may be the two most important new indicators they watch over the next 24 months. They show how many people in the organization are getting the right information, at the right times, to make the best decisions. They measure progress against the enormous hidden costs of working with information. They are a clear measure of the distance between a company's current performance and its full profit potential.

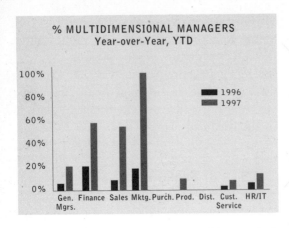

% MULTIDIMENSIONAL MANAGERS
Year-over-Year, YTD

1996
1997

Gen. Finance Sales Mktg. Purch. Prod. Dist. Cust. HR/IT
Mgrs.   Service

WAY 23

Monitoring progress in the number of successful IT partnerships indicates the maturity of information infrastructure in the corporation.

In effect, Way 23 tracks the evolution in the information infrastructure of the company. It is a measure of the number of successful partnerships formed between IT and the management teams of operating departments. The companies who can demonstrate these successful partnerships fastest, will *master information* fastest and be first to gain a core competence in survival.

IT departments often see the full potential of the 24 Ways first because they are used to looking across the entire business. They are also actively looking to partner with business users and respond to their requirements more efficiently. Way 23 allows IT to present an understandable overview of the company's information infrastructure, encourage new partnerships, and position IT's work as a series of successes within a strategic framework.

In addition, each of the 24 Ways — as it is deployed — sets up the baseline targets against which the core competence plan in Way 22 will be measured.

Way 24 — 24 Ways ROI

"Every time we invest in people or information technology, we want to see our ROI. We want to know we are improving performance in the areas that drive our success."

— *Titan Industrial Corporation*

The 24 Ways promise to improve business performance. Way 24 shows the bottom-line impact of each of the 24 Ways on key performance indicators of the business. It answers the question: did performance improve? It shows the value of *mastering information* at every "pressure point" along the supply chain. For example, when a corporation introduces Way 6, *Sales Analysis*, in their sales department, Way 24 will show the impact of performance, as shown in the chart below.

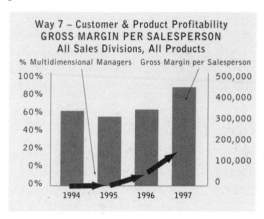

Measuring the impact of the 24 Ways on performance with Way 24.

But something more fundamental is happening as well. Way 24 establishes a relationship between salary, skill, and *output*. It closes the loop between Payroll and HR systems and the key performance indicators in operational systems. The relationship between *skill* and *output* allows management to validate which skills are, in fact, *core competencies* that have a material impact on business. This process of validation confirms the evolutionary plan for the core competence inventory in Way 22. This is the point where corporations gain control over their speed of evolution. Moreover, now that the cost and skills of resources are related to output, multidimensional managers in HR can use this relationship to *predict* business performance.

In Summary

The sweet spots in this chapter *visibly, verifiably, and significantly reduce total operating costs:* they increase both the speed and leverage of understanding information about the corporation's investment in people. In addition, by connecting the cost and skills mix of labor resources directly to output, these sweet spots *enable previously unavailable strategic capabilities.* A corporation can now identify which skills or characteristics are predictors of outcome, and by identifying and tracking their penetration, it can increase the rate of evolution of these critical skills. These new capabilities are *fundamental to developing a core competence in survival.*

The sweet spots in this chapter change the role of HR in corporate mythology. HR managers are no longer simply viewed as the people who make sure that annual performance reviews are carried out and that benefits cards are signed. The information they own and now "master" is too important to the corporation. Their new ability to do price/performance analysis based on job function ratios, skills mix, and salaries gives them a direct role in financial achievement. Imagine a corporation that knows more about its employees than any of its competitors.

Imagine knowing what profile of an employee or what profile of a team has the most impact on profitability. Imagine predicting the profitability of a customer based on the skills composition of the sales team. This is the future for HR... as multidimensional managers.

Way 21 — Human Resource Administration

TIME PERIODS	ORG.	JOB GROUPS	SALARY GRADES	STATUS	LENGTH OF SERVICE	PERF.	INDICATORS
Years	Div	Classes:	Grades	Full Time	<1 Yr	1	# Employees
– – –	– – –	Executives		Part Time	1-2 Yrs	2	# Equiv. FT Staff
Quarters	Depts	Managers		Temp	3-5 Yrs	3	# Perf. Reviews
– – –		Knowledge			5-10 Yrs	4	# Salary Actions
Months		Workers			11-20 Yrs	5	# Promotions
		Admin/Tech			>20 Yrs		Base Salary
		Workers					Incentive Pay
		– – – – –					Benefits Expense
		Job Groups					Tot. Staff Expense
		(Families)					

Way 21 delivers a quick productivity gain in HR's bread-and-butter functions — headcount growth and decline, promotions, and salary administration. Many companies now share subsets of Way 21 directly with operational managers.

Way 22 — Core Competence Inventory

TIME PERIODS	ORG.	BUSINESS SKILL AREA	JOB GROUPS	SALARY GRADES	CORE SKILLS	SKILL RATINGS	INDICATORS
Years	Div	Finance	Classes:	Grades	Technical	Beginner	# of Employees
– – –	– – –	Sales	Executives		Skills	Basic	Skill Rating
Quarters	Depts	Marketing	Managers			Intermed.	(Current)
– – –		Purchasing	Knowledge		Business	Advanced	Skill Rating
Months		Production	Workers		Skills	Expert	(Target)
		Cust. Serv.	Admin/Tech				**Skill Level Gap**
		IT	Workers				# of Skills
		HR	– – – – –				(Current)
		Admin	Job Groups				# of Skills
			(Families)				(Target)
							Skill # Gap

Way 22 transforms the traditional inventory of skills information into analysis of strategic evolution — how departments are using core competencies to drive performance. Plans can be included to show how the skills mix is expected to change over time.

115

Way 23 — BI Deployment

TIME PERIODS	24 WAYS	JOB GROUPS	%MULTI-D MANAGERS	INDICATORS
Years	Departments:	Classes:	0%	# of Employees
– – – – –	Finance	Executives	1–5%	# Multi–D Mgrs.
Quarters	Sales	Managers	6–25%	% Multi–D Mgrs.
	Marketing	Knowledge	26–50%	**% Multi–D Mgrs.**
	Purchasing	Workers	51–75%	**# Ways Deployed**
	Production	Admin/Tech	76–100%	**(Current)**
	Cust. Serv.	Workers		**# Ways Deployed**
	IT	– – – – –		**(Target)**
	HR	Job Groups:		**%Ways Deployed**
	Admin.	Sales Mgrs.		
	– – – – –	Sales Reps		**Potential exception dimension**
	Ways:	Finance		**for 24 Ways Deployment Plan.**
	1–24+	Professionals		
		Etc.		

Way 23 tracks the evolution of business intelligence across the enterprise. It measures the success of IT and business units together in delivering the right information to support key players across the supply chain.

Way 24 — 24 Ways ROI

TIME PERIODS	ORGANIZATION	JOB GROUPS	%MULTI-D MANAGERS	INDICATORS
Years	Divisions	Classes:	0%	Equiv. FT Staff
– – – – –	– – – – –	Executives	1–5%	Staff Expense
Quarters	Departments	Managers	6–25%	Multi–D Mgrs.
– – – –		Knowledge	26–50%	**% Multi–D Mgrs.**
Months		Workers	51–75%	**Sales**
		Admin/Tech	76–100%	**Expense**
		Workers		**Profit**
		– – – – –		**Key Volume Indicators (KVIs)**
		Job Groups:		**Sales/Equiv. FT Staff**
		(Families)		**KVIs/Equiv. FT Staff**

Way 24 measures the bottom-line impact of multidimensional managers. For individual departments, it confirms the impact of each of the 24 Ways on business performance.

Back to the Financial Statements

Income Statement
   Revenue
   COGS
   Gross Profit
   SG&A
   Net Profit

WAYS 21–24

Ways 21–24 have the potential to impact the entire income statement by speeding corporate evolution and predicting productivity based on employee information. At a minimum, they increase the return on administrative investment in Cost of Goods Sold ❶ *and SG&A.* ❷

Chapter 12

The 90-Day Result

The promise of *The Multidimensional Manager* is that any organization can generate strategic cost advantage and increase profitability from many of the 24 Ways within 90 days. Hundreds of corporations have experienced the 90-day result, often to their surprise and often well ahead of their original forecasts. Simply because such results are so unexpected, it is worth explaining how these results were achieved.

Reason 1. The primary enabling technology is low cost and requires minimal training.

All the companies used as examples in *The Multidimensional Manager* used PowerPlay, the market leader in the category of business intelligence software. "The appeal of PowerPlay," reports Howard Dresner of Gartner Group, "is its ease of implementation, management, and use. It's decidedly mass-market business intelligence and can be compared to the fast food industry. Like fast food, PowerPlay is inexpensive and quickly deployed."

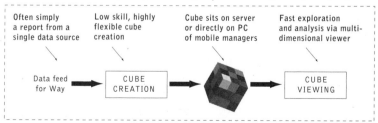

Multidimensional Viewers and Cube Creators are now available in inexpensive software packages.

The quick results are important to IT departments, who are often under pressure in this area. Also, simple, low-cost technology allows corporations to attack several areas — and gain the accumulated benefits — in parallel.

Reason 2. The 24 Ways are designed for lowest common denominator information.

In terms of the availability of information in most corporations, the 24 Ways are designed for the lowest common denominator — particularly Ways 1–5 in finance and the classic *Sales Analysis*, Way 6. The first six of the 24 Ways are designed to operate against single data sources commonly found in manufacturing corporations. Also, it is not necessary to stage the data in an intermediate decision-support database to protect the operational databases, because the multidimensional cubes essentially fulfill that purpose. As a result, it is unnecessary to queue up behind data warehousing projects that may be underway in the corporation.

We are often asked how the 24 Ways fit into data warehousing initiatives, since they may be a corporation's main ongoing project to get better information to corporate managers.

First, it's worth noting that in 1995, the average data warehouse took three years to complete and cost over $3 million according to METAGroup (the analysts who specialize in the data warehouse market). Because of the cost, timeframe, magnitude, and attendant risk of these projects, many data warehouse initiatives are never completed.

We are convinced that corporations have to get meaningful information to managers in a much shorter time period, with much lower cost, and at much lower risk. The 24 Ways achieves each of these objectives, while complementing any warehouse initiative. If a data warehouse exists, the 24 Ways can certainly take advantage of any important data that's in it.

If a data warehouse doesn't exist but a project is in process, the 24 Ways will most likely accelerate its completion and reduce its risk of failure. Data warehouse projects tend to be over-generous in selecting the data to be inventoried. The overly broad selection of data delays the project, increases the cost, and dilutes the return on investment. The 24 Ways program tends to shorten this delay by encouraging organizations to focus first on the inventory of data that has a proven impact on income statements and balance sheets.

Also, data warehouse projects uncover an ugly truth. They reveal that much of the data held in operational systems by corporations is incorrect. The reason is often that operational business units who could correct it have never had the opportunity to see it. According to John Parkinson, Chief Technologist, Connected Enterprise Solutions, Ernst & Young LLP, 50 percent of the legacy data in some mainframe systems is so inaccurate it's not worth cleaning — or keeping. Now the major problem for the data warehouse project becomes cleaning and correcting the data that's destined for the warehouse. But how is that done efficiently when only the users know if and when the data is correct?

The 24 Ways proves a surprisingly effective solution to this problem. The most important information from operational systems is funneled directly off the systems into multidimensional cubes. Multidimensional managers in operational departments quickly explore their cubes, notice incorrect facts, and pressure their departments to make corrections. The departments correct the operational systems as part of their normal data-entry procedures. Now, the corrected data can flow into any ongoing warehouse project.

Reason 3. An organization can start anywhere in the 24 Ways.

The third reason a 90-day result is achievable is that an organization can start almost anywhere in the 24 Ways. There are no dependencies and there is no required sequence of events. You don't have to do Way 1 in finance before you do Way 18 in customer service. If equipment downtime in plants is the biggest issue facing management this week, a corporation can start there.

A company can turn on "green lights" in the 24 Ways scorecard in any order. Any "green light" improves the company's cost structure and sustainable competitive advantage. And any "green light" initiates the feedback loop that corrects the data in that part of the company.

In short, no substantial economic or technological barrier stands in the way of getting at least one Way up and running within 90 days.

How It Gets Done in Your Organization

In our experience with corporations and the 24 Ways, success always depends on someone who lights up, sees the potential, and decides to make it happen in his or her organization. We call this person the BI Champion.

Interestingly, and unlike the situation with most reengineering projects, the BI Champion doesn't need to be at the top of the organization. The BI Champion could literally be anywhere in the organization. Sometimes the BI Champion is in the business unit, sometimes in the IT organization. In any case, wherever BI Champions are, they tend to rise rapidly in the organization because their work is quickly seen to have unusual value.

Also, BI Champions don't require executive sponsorship to get started. Their first task — often self-appointed — is to create a small, committed team with at least two members. One member represents the business unit and understands the business need. The other member represents IT and understands where the data is and how to get it. The BI Champion is often one of the two team members.

Getting any of the 24 Ways up and running involves a very simple conversation within the team. The conversation is simple because any Way can be described in a single table of dimensions and indicators. We've shown these tables as illustrations throughout this book. Each table defines the sweet spot for a Way.

TIME PERIODS	ORGANIZATIONS	PRODUCTS	CUSTOMERS	INDICATORS
Years	Sales Divisions	Prod Lines	Top 100	Revenue
- - - - -	- - - - - - - - -	- - - - - -	- - - - -	Units
Quarters	Sales Districts	Brands	Other	Discount
- - - - -	- - - - - - - -	- - - - -		Discount %
Months	Sales Reps	Products		Avg. Selling Price
- - - - -		- - - - -		
YTD		SKUs		
Prior YTD				
QTD				
Prior QTD				
Current Month				
Prior Month				

There are only two important questions: (1) Does this information have value to the business users? (2) Can IT get the data?

The conversation centers on two important questions. Will the information in the table have value for the business users? (Are these the right dimensions? Does each dimension go down to the right level in the organization for decision-making? Are the right indicators included?) Once it is clear that the dimensions and indicators have value, the second question is whether IT can get the data. If the answer is positive, then the team may be as little as a few hours away from a result.

Going operational will obviously require a higher level of departmental sponsorship. But a working example of one of the 24 Ways is usually all a BI Champion needs to rally a sponsor. At that point there are only two important actions:

Set a 90-day deadline.

Make your deadline.

The results will show in the Annual Report the next time it is published for the board, the bank, and the investment community.

The 24 Ways and Beyond

Great principles such as Clauswitz's "concentration of resources" and Vilfredo Pareto's "80/20 rule" are obvious once they are pointed out. The same is true with business reengineering. Once you notice where a business process is broken, it's obvious that it should be fixed. The business process of getting information to key managers across the supply chain is clearly broken in most corporations today.

By capturing the success of many innovative companies, we have tried to eliminate the risk that fixing a business process often implies. Michael Hammer and James Champy, who wrote the 1993 classic *Reengineering the Corporation*, defined business reengineering as:

> *"The fundamental rethinking and radical redesign of business processes to achieve dramatic improvements in critical, contemporary measures of performance, such as cost, quality, service and speed."*

The 24 Ways has done the *fundamental rethinking* and the *radical redesign*. We have attempted to make the 24 Ways a commodity. Any manufacturing corporation today can literally peel off the cellophane, apply the 24 Ways, and see dramatic improvement.

Multidimensional managers are the new unit of competitive advantage. They are the new samurai in corporations — the new warrior class. They have better ROI characteristics. They have a cost-of-working-with-information advantage over their predecessors. They have new X-ray vision for the factors that drive the indicators they manage. They have superior alignment around corporate goals.

In our experience, individuals who become multidimensional managers frequently accelerate their careers and certainly accelerate the progress of their departments. They gain greater control over their areas of responsibility, and therefore achieve a greater sense of mastery and accomplishment in their work.

The first corporations to turn on the 24 Ways and unleash multidimensional managers across their organizations will drive the cost structures in their industries.

There are no ultimate winners in the race to succeed in business. But if history is any measure, corporations get squeezed out of the race at an alarming rate. Survival in the marathon is a matter of *strategic cost advantage* and *profitability*. It's a matter of getting fresh runners into the race. It's a matter of developing a core competence in survival. It's a matter of everyone understanding their impact on the financial statements. The financial statements are the final scorecard. They record every corporation's position in the marathon. With the 24 Ways, you can change that position in 90 days.

About the Authors

The authors of *The Multidimensional Manager* are pioneers in the development of business intelligence technology and applications.

Dr. Richard A. Connelly, the President of Business Intelligence International, has worked on the front line of designing and implementing information systems for more than 25 years. His work at the Chase Manhattan Bank, CIGNA, and the Hay Group has involved him in personally managing all of the issues covered in the 24 Ways. His multidimensional systems for investment industry service analysis and steel industry supply chain management are used globally. Dr. Connelly is a graduate of the University of Notre Dame and Michigan State University.

Robin McNeill was the product champion from 1990 to 1995 for PowerPlay, the multidimensional software marketed by Cognos Incorporated. During that period, PowerPlay emerged as the popular choice of multidimensional managers at all levels of responsibility. Mr. McNeill's work in developing business intelligence tools has placed him in the forefront of consulting to leading Fortune 1000 companies.

As Vice President, Product Marketing, at Cognos, Mr. McNeill continues to drive the development of software at Cognos from customer experience, isolating the behavior patterns of corporate managers and then matching Cognos software to those behaviors. He is a graduate of the Royal Military College of Canada.

Roland P. Mosimann is in charge of Business Intelligence International's operations. His business and consulting experience has included advance marketing and strategy assignments in Europe, Asia, and North America. A former consultant at McKinsey & Company, Mr. Mosimann has also served as a member of the Executive Board of the World Economic Forum in Geneva, Switzerland. He was responsible for leading the financial services and transportation management sectors of the Forum's activities, working with executive officers and government officials in North America, Europe, and Asia. He is a graduate of the London School of Economics and the Wharton School at the University of Pennsylvania.

As partners in BI International Inc., Dr. Connelly and Mr. Mosimann offer a *BI University* in Philadelphia and London to teach the 24 Ways to business managers. Using a computer-simulated version of the 24 Ways, business managers create a multi-year plan for a manufacturing business, then run the business using the 24 Ways to optimize results. BI International also provides services that enable managers to plan and track 24 Ways implementation progress. These services include testing and certification of the 24 Ways business skills for multidimensional managers and implementors across the organization.

Acknowledgments

The authors would like to acknowledge the many outstanding individuals and companies who have contributed to the publication of *The Multidimensional Manager*. First are the creative individuals and their corporations who invented the 24 Ways. They are the real authors of the book. Only a subset are specifically mentioned in this book, but since these discoveries are often carefully guarded, we would like especially to thank the companies who agreed to share their experience publicly. Many other managers in these companies were obviously involved, but here are the individuals who worked with us directly:

Doug Conety, Air Products and Chemicals, Inc.; *Bill Lawson*, AMETEK, Inc.; *Paul Walsh* and *Steve Oberlander*, Analog Devices, Inc.; *Bill Stein, Stephen Woodward,* and *Ronald Juncal*, Armstrong World Industries, Inc.; *Eric Brassard*, Avon Canada Inc.; *Don Waddell*, Chevron Products Co.; *Greg Bergin,* Compaq Computer Corporation; *Scott Schultz* and *Janet Wendelken*, Coors Brewing Company; *Art Asnen*, Crown, Cork & Seal Company, Inc.; *George Bablis*, Domtar Inc.; *Jim Trebilock*, Dr Pepper/Seven Up, Inc.; *Harmik Baghadasarian* and *Janette Reynolds*, Epson America, Inc.; *Jeff Tietz*, Fellowes Manufacturing Co.; *Paul Bilowicz*, Glaxo Wellcome Inc.; *Terry Doyle*, H. J. Heinz Company of Canada Ltd.; *Richard Wittich* and *Chris Ayers*, Hamilton Beach/Proctor-Silex, Inc.; *Glenn Pettigrew* and *Dan MacLeod*, Maritime Tel & Tel Limited; *Mark Zozulia*, Moen Incorporated; *Els Olthof,* PTT Telecom BV; *Tom Arrowood* and *Harold Hoffman*, The Budd Company; *John Baron, Michael Levin,* and *Craig Morritt*, Titan Industrial Corporation; *Bob Lawson*, Tropitone Inc.; *Kathy Carpenter*, Unifi, Inc.; *Arthur Greenberg*, Witco Corporation; and *Gordon Khan* and *Orville Trembly*, York International Corporation.

We are grateful for the work of *Andrew S. Grove*, CEO of Intel Corporation, in *High Output Management* (Random House 1993). His application of manufacturing principles to manager productivity is a foundation of *The Multidimensional Manager*.

We wish to acknowledge *Geoffrey Moore*, *Crossing the Chasm* (HarperBusiness 1991), for his classic description of the three "must-have value propositions" for pragmatic buyers:

"It enables a previously unavailable strategic capability in an area of prime operational focus; it radically improves productivity on an already well-understood critical success factor; and it visibly, verifiably, and significantly reduces total overall operating costs."

We also want to thank *Howard Dresner* of Gartner Group, who invented the term Business Intelligence and who has supported the authors and many of the principles of the 24 Ways over the past years.

Finally, we would like to thank our editorial team of *Opher Banarie, Stephanie Bigusiak, Jim Cassidy, Judy Cushing, Cynthia Incze, Gordon McMillan, and Alan Rottenberg*, for their insistence on clarity; *Kamal Jobanputra* for his refinements to the 24 Ways; and *Sylvie Pelletier* for the cover and page design of the book.

229484